The Sooner You Laugh the Faster You Heal

How to Challenge the Assumptions that Ruin Your Life

Anne Barab

The Sooner You Laugh the Faster You Heal
Copyright © 2014 by Anne Barab

ISBN 978-1-940170-38-1

Printed in USA by 48HrBooks (www.48HrBooks.com)

Dedication

To Stu, Whitney, Lauren and Mandala

Thank you for being the wind beneath my bat wings

Table of Contents

Introduction

"Laughter makes life richer."
Anne Barab

Laughter makes life richer. It's also the absolute best way to express and eliminate anxiety. And YOU are your own best target.

On the following pages, we'll poke fun at our common yet ridiculous assumptions imbedded in the serious business of relationships, parenting, cancer, work, travel, aging, complaining, speaking, laundry, exercising and Jerry Springer.

Take lifelong relationships… please. No wait, what I mean is: maintaining a relationship with an unrelated person until you're dead takes more than puppy love, mainly because unexamined assumptions create most of our unhappiness and disappointments.

Relationship expectations are constantly reinforced by the fantasy culture of movies, TV, and lengthy chats with girl friends. Some of these assumptions include:

- My spouse is supposed to make me happy.

- True Love is easy. If it's not easy, then it's not True Love.

- We've lost the "magic."

- I deserve to be happy.

If you've ever said any of these things, or even thought them, then you DESPERATELY NEED to read this book.

What you think "ought to be" is frequently irrational and often comical, but there you are with your shorts all twisted up in a knot over an impossible expectation. Fix what you think "ought to be" and you fix your relationships, your happiness and your success.

When things are tough, we respond in one of three ways:

1. Change the situation.

2. Change nothing.

3. Change yourself.

This book is not about changing the situation by making others do the changing. Expecting everybody else to do the heavy lifting sounds like this: "It's all your fault!" "I quit!" "I want a divorce!" "We're putting you up for adoption!"

This book is also not about changing nothing and just blunting the pain. That's victimhood and its theme song is "Why me?" We're all victimhood experts; we just use different pain killers like alcohol, drugs, work, adultery, food, TV, porn, internet, video games – the list goes on...

This book is definitely not for you if:

1. You really enjoy being crabby and unhappy. You may not realize you're toxic, but others around you do. Just ask them.

2. You blame your partner, your boss, your kids, or your circumstances for your unhappiness.

3. You can't laugh at yourself.

If that description fits you, I beg you to PUT THIS BOOK DOWN AND STEP AWAY FROM THE SHELF!

You're not going to learn anything because you never do and frankly, I don't want this book added to your ever growing list of stuff to complain about.

This book is about changing yourself.

It's the unconscious junk in your head that creates your problems. We'll illuminate some of these assumptions, laugh at their absurdity, readjust your mindset and heal what hurts.

If you've suffered through tough times and you're ready to stop the pain, then this book definitely IS for you.

I've been there. I know how it feels. I'm happily married to the love of my life, but it hasn't always been that way. We were soooo happy on our wedding day, but then inevitably things started going downhill – roughly five minutes after we drove away from the church.

The reason was because we went into marriage with wildly differing and equally unrealistic expectations.

I thought we would come home from work and over a candlelit dinner we'd endlessly share our deepest innermost feelings and every little detail of the day. His deepest emotion was "I feel hungry."

I expected complete emotional support. He expected live-in maid service and sex.

In a moment of abject misery, I made a list of my Beloved's pros and cons. There were jillions of nit-picky criticisms on the cons side, and only one pro. "He makes me laugh." A mate who can make you laugh is worth keeping.

That was 43 years ago. We like to think of our marriage as the happiest 37 years of our lives. The way we've learned to survive and then really thrive is through laughing – mainly at ourselves and our silly assumptions about how things "ought to be."

We've discovered this practice works wonders in facing the daunting challenges of keeping a relationship together for centuries, raising kids to become taxpayers, confronting workplace frustrations, thriving with cancer, re-inventing ourselves and our marriage, exploring the world with a sense of wonder, grand parenting with gusto and growing old but not cranky.

Yes, broken relationships hurt. Yes, kids disappoint you. Yes, jobs suck. Yes, life hasn't turned out the way you thought it should.

If you're ready to laugh about the unconscious assumptions that keep you painfully paralyzed, then keep reading, start laughing at yourself and let the healing begin.

Anne Barab
May, 2014

Fall in Love with the
One You Married

*"A successful marriage requires falling in love
many times, always with the same person."*
Mignon McLaughlin

Long lasting relationships are the most valuable commodity on earth. They're also quite rare, primarily because they require unrelated people to get along with each other until they're dead.

Relationships are generally composed of two different components, mainly a woman who is looking for Prince Charming, a life partner who will ceaselessly adore her, with whom to reproduce perfect little clones of themselves, someone to share laughter and tears, good times and bad while always remaining young and alluring like lovers in movies, a soul mate who can read her mind, surprise her with fabulous gifts and shower her with love and companionship.

The other component, the man wants casual conversation leading to sex.

In the beginning the complex feelings of attraction make participants feel giddy and light-headed. You can't stand to be apart; you think, dream, eat and sleep in a haze of intense fascination with the other person. You're alternately full of anticipation and desire, then despondent or lost when you're apart. Unfortunately, these are also the symptoms of obsessive-compulsive disorder.

First Comes Love

If you're the female, you spend long hours writing Mr. and Mrs. Sturdy P. Berger, Ms. Elaine Berger, Mrs. Sturdy Berger, Elaine and Sturdy Berger, Sturdy and Elaine Berger. Then you branch out into the whole hyphenated name dilemma: Elaine MacDonald-Berger, Elaine Berger-MacDonald, Mrs. Sturdy MacDonald-Berger, Mr. and Mrs. Sturdy P. MacDonald-Berger, etc. all surrounded with little hearts.

You dream about little Sturdy Jr. and his precious baby sister Inez MacDonald-Berger. You imagine a darling starter house with cute curtains, bright sunny rooms and a big back yard full of flowers and a wooden swing set with children running and laughing.

Then of course, as Sturdy Sr. becomes more successful, there'll be the Big House, a showy Georgian manor with rolling lawns and limos driving up to deposit beautiful people in diaphanous garments for the spring garden party. Yes, life with Sturdy will surely be the stuff of your dreams.

If you're the guy, you're watching sports and vaguely wondering when you'll have sex again. You also dream of tickets to the World Series.

Yes, men and women enter relationships with differing expectations. Scientists say the obsessive-compulsive disorder, which many people call "love," wears off after about two years. If you've been living together before the wedding that magic elixir called "love" will disappear and boredom will set in roughly five minutes after the ceremony.

But you're stuck, so you plunge ahead with the relationship – unless of course you're a Kardashian in which case you file for divorce during the reception.

Back in the olden days a girl was supposed to keep herself "pure" for her wedding night. There were two reasons for this custom:

a) It was in accordance with Biblical teachings that apparently a new car is more valuable than a used clunker AND

2) The hope for sex was the only way to get a guy to commit.

Frankly, I don't know how any woman today gets a man to the altar, what with the cookie jar being fully explored before the nuptials.

Then Comes Marriage

Post ceremony the fun really begins because you're in it deep and F-O-R-E-V-E-R, but no pressure. As a newly married couple you can party till dawn, sleep late, travel at will and just generally maintain a carefree and exuberant lifestyle of nonstop good times knowing that somewhere down the road the ball and chain of "children" and "responsibility" and "soccer" are going to destroy your existence.

My Beloved Stu (spell check returns "stud") is an electrical engineer and the love of my life even though we are total and complete opposites.

I'm 5'1" outgoing, chatty, and materialistic, what with constantly shopping for the next pair of shoes that will truly change my life. He's 6'2", slim, quiet, conservative and persnickety.

We stayed suspended in the nether world of DINKS (Dual Income No Kids) for ten years before reproducing. It took us that long AFTER the ceremony to actually commit to the relationship. For the first seven years we were just going steady.

My commitment-phobic Beloved did not believe in acquiring possessions because they would just be something to argue over in the divorce. So in the beginning we lived in a charming unfurnished apartment resplendent in orange shag carpet (it was the seventies) with nothing but a bed, a desk and a TV. At some point we also acquired two avocado green lawn chairs for living room furniture so we could entertain.

Eventually our marriage deepened into a connection capable of sustaining joint property ownership in the form of a house. Then at last we eternally yoked ourselves together through the breeding process.

Then Comes a Baby Carriage

Kids bring a whole new dimension into the relationship. Creating the first child signifies the last time the two of you will enjoy lusty and unrestrained sex for the better part of two decades.

Actually I take that back. When you say, "Hey dear, let's make a baby tonight and irrevocably change our lives forever" sexual desire tends to wilt.

Engineers employ a very effective form of birth control – their personality. But at length and at last we overcame that hurdle.

We brought forth our firstborn and wrapped him in a blue swaddle and laid him in a bassinette by our bed – then promptly moved him to the bathroom and closed the door, then repositioned him down the hall in his adorable nursery and ultimately fantasized about putting him out in the garage so we could get some sleep.

Our first child was born in July of 1980 which was the hottest Dallas summer during the entire 20th century. I swore I'd never have another baby in July and I didn't.

We had two babies in August.

We didn't know there were two babies in there until ten days before they were born, but there were signs. We just ignored them.

When you're pregnant, people ask you one of two questions. First they politely inquire "When are you due?" meaning "I see by your size that you have a ways to go."

But then at some point you reach a certain critical mass roughly the size of a cement truck and the question changes to "How much longer?" meaning "Please stand back in case your water breaks."

I was only four months along and a lady in my company cafeteria asked me the latter question "How much longer?" When I replied that I still had five months to go and she spewed Pepsi through her nose.

Then my Beloved observed that I resembled the Goodyear Blimp, which I thought was hysterical. So hand in hand we purchased a size XXL maternity shirt and printed GOODYEAR across the apex.

During the ninth month that shirt was the only garment capable of covering my pulchritude. The way we knew the babies had dropped was when GOODYEAR moved up.

Lumbering out of the bank a week before delivery, an approaching man slapped his thigh and croaked, "I just love a fat lady with a sense of humor!"

Laughing about the tough stuff helps.

There were days I really wanted to run away from home because we had three babies in diapers. Our two year old son Jeff refused to potty train. He claimed the changing table was the only place he got any quality time.

Children really tend to dampen the intimate aspects of a relationship. For a while the new mother's chest is sexually inoperative due to spurting like a fire hydrant. Her body emits the lingering fragrance of breast milk, spit up, and poop. Combine that with extreme sleep deprivation and sexual satisfaction is achieved if the woman is semi-conscious at the beginning.

Okay, so sex becomes occasional, like Haley's Comet, but you still have each other and the blessings of your growing familial unit.

At this point the marital affiliation is less about affection and more like the Iditarod race with you and your beloved harnessed together as huskies in the traces and the musher is the Grim Reaper and the sled is your house and the luggage is all the kids, pets, and vehicles that you, as the dog sled team, drag around behind you. The concept of "True Love" begins to wear thin.

True Love

What do young people today think about true love? According to the Urban Dictionary (which by its name must mean it contains "new" and less old fashioned, more up-to-date clarifications of words) defines "True Love" as (Good Lord, I am copying this verbatim. God save us all.) "not wanting to go anywhere without her, not caring what other people think about the two of u, when u feel depressed and sickly when ur not with her, u feel like ur life has no meaning or purpose without her, and that if she wasn't holding ur hand u would float away to heaven from where she came. Love is wanting to marry her even tho ya'll haven't been dating that long. Love is the feeling you get when all you have to do is think of her and it brings a smile to ur face and a yourning to your heart. Love is not being able to think about nething but her…"

I'm not making this drivel up. Clearly the author never passed grammar school English or for that matter experienced a relationship lasting longer than prom night.

No, this is the part of life where love has practically nothing to do with preserving the relationship.

This is the part where iron clad Commitment maintains the union.

"Love" is just an emotion that comes and goes, much like indigestion.

In the middle of this marathon, the weak of heart may falter. Remember Elaine imagining picket fences and rosy-cheeked cherubs with Sturdy? Well, now she's thinking things like: "Sturdy doesn't make me happy anymore" or "I deserve to be happy and he's not it" or "We've lost the magic."

Are we talking about a mature relationship or Disneyland?

Thirteen years into the marriage Elaine and Sturdy hit the wall. Or more accurately, Elaine hits the wall. Sturdy is watching sports at the time.

Elaine drags Sturdy to counseling.

In the therapist's office, Elaine pours out her heart and soul about how Sturdy doesn't do this and that, and how disenchanted she is and how they just argue about money and "the bills" (mysterious expenditures that materialize from whence no one knows) and how he always has time for golf but never for the kids and her, and how he doesn't appreciate her and all she does for the kids, the house, and the family, and she's lonely because he just comes home and plunks down in his Barcalounger, code named The Cone of Silence, where she's not allowed to interrupt unless the house is on fire and she's sick and tired of being sick and tired and quid pro quo being what's expected he'd better seriously shape up or she's leaving.

Sturdy listens quietly and then responds with a shockingly simple statement. "Elaine, I'm not responsible for making you happy."

The therapist agrees.

Elaine is stupefied.

Deep in her reptilian brain Elaine had always thought making your mate happy was part of the marriage contract – to love, honor, obey and MAKE YOUR BELOVED HAPPY!

Wasn't it even an actual law – like one of those unalienable rights she had to memorize in seventh grade… the right to pursue Life, Liberty, and your partner's Happiness?

This is indeed a distressing turn of events. Elaine rails out against the injustice, the ignorance, the unfairness of it all. After months of counseling, several medications, and an inordinate quantity of time spent talking with girl friends, going over every little detail, rehashing every miniscule hurt and offense, Elaine finally gets tired of listening to herself complain.

In a blinding flash of insight she reasons, "Hey, maybe I should take responsibility for my own happiness!"

Falling Back in Love

Elaine sets to work "falling back in love" with Sturdy. First she makes a T Chart of his Pros and Cons. The Cons drone on for three pages single spaced listing things like:

- Didn't put his clothes in the hamper in Spring of '96

- Doesn't wash the dishes before putting them in the dishwasher like I told him

- Never offers to do the laundry

- Interrupts me to tell me what I should do to fix things

- Never shares his deepest innermost feelings with me

Upon reflection Elaine realizes that:

- She's expected Sturdy to be her "girl friend."

- She doesn't want to be married to a "girl friend" because a real girl friend would want 50% of the talk time and expect her to be "interested" in her inane and boring stuff and she,

Elaine, really doesn't want to share 50/50 because she much prefers the 90% air time she currently experiences.

- Sturdy's deepest innermost feelings can be summed up as "Huh?"

Pros consisted of one entry: He makes me laugh.

Elaine thinks a man who can make her laugh is worth a second chance.

Then she writes down the characteristics of her ideal mate:

- Caring husband
- Great father
- Excellent provider
- Trustworthy
- Kind
- Thoughtful
- Dependable

Sturdy is beginning to look downright sexy.

Armed with a little introspection, a lot of common sense, and a sprinkling of newfound wisdom, Elaine falls back in love with her dream guy.

In our disposable relationship culture we're encouraged to solve relationship problems by discarding partners like yesterday's underwear. There's a pervasive attitude that if you're not pleasing me, entertaining me, meeting my needs, then this obviously isn't "true love" and I'll just trade you in on a different model with presumably better feature/functions.

These escapist assumptions that the next fantasy relationship will be perfect create huge amounts of heartache, suffering and collateral damage in the form of divorces, children of divorce, split property, anger, depression, and revenge. And absolutely awful reality television shows.

Elaine decides that loving right trumps finding the right love. Perhaps she had the right love all along anyway.

And that's how long-term adult relationships survive.

Falling Back in Love Again

Time passes.

Sturdy Jr. and Inez grow up and go out into the wide, wide world to seek their fortunes. Elaine shakes off empty nest blues by starting a successful business selling whatchamacallits. Sturdy cuts back to working only 50 hours a week, and plays lots of golf. They drift apart.

The relationship hits another trough.

Elaine, always the emotional weather vane of the partnership, hosts a state-of-the-union meeting with Sturdy in which she explains in a deadly quiet voice that:

1. Last time she stayed with him for the children's sake AND

2. Because she needed his money and the security it provided, BUT

3. Since she is a now successful woman of independent means AND

4. She did not work this hard to stay slim, attractive and interesting just to be ignored SO

5. Since she is the best trophy wife he's ever going to have AND

6. The only thing he's bringing to the relationship right now is his personality WHICH

7. For the last few years has been remarkably deficient SO NOW

8. He'd better up level his game OR

9. She is OUT of this sham of a marriage.

Sturdy is surprised – on a number of levels.

- First, seeing as how he spends most of his free time either asleep, golfing or safely ensconced in The Cone of Silence, he is totally unaware that she has been experiencing dissatisfaction.

- Second, he hasn't previously noticed that she now makes a substantial amount of money.

- Third, he comprehends at a cellular level that the rules of the game have changed.

- Fourth, he realizes he much prefers the comfort and security of his Elaine-based lifestyle, because

- Fifth, he has neither the energy nor the money to attract, maintain and service a younger and more demanding "Trophy Wife."

- Sixth, he is stimulated and sexually aroused by this fiery woman.

Sturdy takes Elaine right there on the den floor, proudly sustaining major rug burns in the process.

As a result of rekindled intimacy, this couple opens the next chapter of their lives.

He loses 50 pounds. She, with the services of a hormone pellet, welcomes long lost sexual desire back into her life. Together they take up yoga, meditation and square dancing.

They cease considering Hamburger Helper cuisine and begin experimenting with exotic new recipes such as Spicy Thai Lobster Soup and Hearts of Palm with Green Tea-Noodle Salad.

They build a deck in the back yard and start inviting people over for wine, cheese, smoked salmon and capers.

They travel. They hold hands. They cuddle and kiss. They laugh a lot. And at last, in the act of ultimate trust and adoration, they share the remote.

And that's how long-lasting relationships thrive.

Relationship Killing Assumptions

ASSUMPTION #1: It's my spouse's job to make me happy.

Wrong. Happiness is 50% genetics, 40% choice and only 10% circumstances. So if you ditch this partner, you're still hauling 90% of the problem with you into the next relationship – and the next – and the next one too. Happiness is a choice not a circumstance. Choose to be happy.

ASSUMPTION #2: True Love is easy. If it's not easy then it's not "True Love."

Wrong. True Love is obsessive compulsive behavior that begins settling down into full-grown affection and companionship in about two years. Chasing after those excited feelings of infatuation is like being trapped forever in junior high school purgatory.

ASSUMPTION #3: We've lost the magic.

There is no magic (see True Love above.) Hopefully both partners grow, mature and change. Plus you get distracted with kids, career and stuff. Marriage is not a mythical fairy tale. It's a lifetime partnership signified by jewelry.

ASSUMPTION #4: I deserve to be happy.

Sure you do. So quit blaming your partner and take responsibility for your own happiness. See above.

ASSUMPTION #5: It's not possible to fall back in love with the same person.

Yes, it is. If you married a person of quality, the quality is still there. Like a dog that hides a bone, go dig it up and start appreciating the value of your mate all over again.

Relationship Saving Actions

ACTION #1: Make a realistic assessment of your discontents.

It's true that making a list of pros and cons will help you see your root dissatisfaction. Cons will always outnumber pros because it takes no skill to see the negative. As human beings we are hard wired to look for threats to our survival.

When you refocus by looking for the positive traits, you will be amazed and delighted by the rediscovered treasure of your beloved.

ACTION #2: Listen intently to each other.

Ladies, if you married the strong, silent type then quit expecting him to be your "girl friend." Men are remarkably communicative when they sense sex on the horizon, i.e. dating. Do him a favor and call a friend if you absolutely, positively MUST vent for the better part of several days.

Guys, just listen – without the TV remote in your quivering fingers. Focus, look her in the eye and DON'T interrupt. She just wants to process her thoughts by telling you the story.

Set the egg timer for at least three minutes before interrupting to tell her how to "solve her problem."

Apply all the expensive "communication and leadership skills" they taught you to use on the J.O.B.

ACTION #3: What do I really want?

In any situation people can identify what they don't want. It's generally whatever is directly in front of them at the moment. Much harder is the clarity to identify what you DO want.

If you married a person of quality you probably made a good choice and s/he actually personifies what you DO want. Real "True Love" flourishes when you quit harping about boredom and complaining that "we don't have anything in common anymore."

Real "True Love" builds character – the moral fiber to trudge through the mediocre times, tough it out in the bad times, and muster the creativity and persistence it takes to restore good times.

Most marriages "fail" because the partners get lazy, neglectful and just plain quit. As our heroine Elaine discovered, loving right trumps finding the right love.

One of the most rewarding and enriching components of long-lasting relationships is shared history.

When you idealistically vow to stay together "for better or worse" you have no idea how painful and character-building "worse" is going to be. Every relationship encounters potholes in the road. It's how you respond that rips you apart or bonds you together.

The pain of unhappy times, the personal growth, the rediscovery of cherished traits in your mate, the ebb and flow of anger, forgiveness and joy, the steadfast dedication to the partnership and the person – this is the stuff of "True Love."

It is a richly rewarding journey that demands your complete commitment and the best you've got to offer in this lifetime experimental project.

And a thriving long term relationship is totally worth it.

Loving right trumps
finding the right love

I Forbid You to Call Me a Control Freak

"Helicopter parents pay extremely close attention to a child's experiences and problems, particularly at educational institutions.
They hover overhead like helicopters."
Wikipedia

Many of life's frustrations stem from the notion that we can control the people and situations around us. The foolhardiness of this attitude sank in on me only after I began to reproduce.

Ah, the joys of parenting! In the beginning, two totally untrained, utterly unprepared adultish individuals birth an innocent little baby who has no idea he is being issued to people who couldn't possibly pass a babysitting test.

But in spite of this, the hospital allows these bunglers to take home the poor unfortunate baby whom they have named Elroy Cyrell Stickle, a name which clearly illustrates their parenting incompetence.

It is the miracle of life that many first born children survive the well meaning ineptitude of their parents.

First born infants are changed, nursed, burped, bathed, rocked, cuddled, held, sung to and just generally pampered to exhaustion. Frequently they rise up in their cribs screaming "Please leave me alone so I can get some sleep!"

But their ever-vigilant parents misinterpret these sobs as a desperate appeal for more attention so they pick up their baby and recommence the changing, nursing, burping, bathing, rocking, cuddling cycle all over again.

Firstborns are also subjected to hideous garments, many of which were received at the adorably themed baby shower. In fact, firstborns own so many miniature outfits that they must change clothes every 15 minutes in order to wear them all before they outgrow them. Thereafter, their doting mommies purchase large quantities of cute rompers decorated with embroidered bunnies, puppies, and chicks accompanied by the words "Mommy's Lil' Angel."

Firstborns are extensively photographed. A mere two weeks old, little Elroy Cyrell sleeps through his first professional photo session, costing more than bridal portraiture, where he is propped up in a variety of precious poses.

But that's only the beginning. His parents click endless candids of him nursing, sleeping, bathing, pooping, strapped into his car seat, sitting in his high chair, eating cereal, drinking from a sippy cup, crawling, pulling up, staggering his first drunken sailor steps and smearing his first birthday cupcake all over himself.

In fact, little Elroy never actually sees his parents' faces because they are always obstructed by their cell phones snapping photos of him then texting them out to relatives and their closest 13,487 Facebook friends.

Such is the life of first born babies. Second and third born children plus the remainder of the human race wear poopy diapers upwards of three days, sport raggedy hand-me-down clothing and are photographed infrequently, like the day they come home from the hospital and the day they graduate from high school. Also, they're generally more normal.

Hover Parenting

Today's parents are not just the clueless newbies that prior generations were. They're worse because they hover over their children, attempting to control every teeny tiny little element of their child's life.

Frequently women have sonograms the morning after conception to determine the baby's sex so they can name him or her and immediately apply to the most exclusive private nursery schools.

I'd say lighten up, all you really intense parents, especially when your child reaches about 30 years old.

Generally the moms are more intense than dads. But dads express their hover love most frequently at youth sporting events by yelling obscenities at their kids, the coach, the opposing team, and even passing traffic much, like a barking dog. The more competitive the dad, the more "hover love" he showers on his child.

Moms show their hover love through acts of maintenance, such as wiping up various and sundry body substances, cutting the child's food into little molecular-sized portions, telling them their garments are unacceptable, and shrieking at teachers.

The problem with hover parents is they think controlling everything in their child's universe will produce full grown, adult-like individuals that obediently fulfill all the parents' wishes.

Unfortunately, what they frequently manufacture instead are robotic, weak, sniveling, useless, and extremely angry ax murderers.

Whoa! Don't you think that's a bit of a jump? Yes, I do. So no ax murderers, mainly because these kids were never allowed to handle sharp objects. Round tip scissor murderers, maybe.

Toddlerhood is a time when control-freak, hover parents really shine because it's a high maintenance phase requiring little maturity or emotional intelligence on their part.

These parents also do pretty well during the elementary school years when, in addition to child maintenance, they take on PTA, fundraising and carpooling little Elroy and his friends to all their activities.

Hover parents' biggest challenge is "processing" the endless stream of school papers coming home in their child's backpack, papers that take up residence on the kitchen counter, wallpaper the refrigerator and appear to wantonly reproduce overnight.

By "process" I mean critique the teacher's handwriting, complain that the assignments are too difficult – or too easy, discover that Elroy got an F for not turning in his homework, call the principal to weave an intricate web of excuses for Elroy, and oh yes, demand the teacher's immediate dismissal.

Adolescence

It's when kids reach adolescence that all hell breaks loose for hover parents. One evening mom and dad tenderly kiss cherubic Elroy Cyrell and his angelic little sister Margaret goodnight. The next morning they discover their children's bodies are inhabited by aliens that snarl and glower at parental guidance.

Actually it's not aliens that manifest this unpleasant change. Its hormones, gallons of them sloshing around on the inside of these formerly adorable miniature humans that transforms them into unsightly, smelly, pimple-infested creatures who slam doors, constantly text their friends and subsist on a steady diet of energy drinks and Cheetos.

Here's the deal. Children change. The only question is: will their parents adapt to the change?

That's the funny thing about hover parents. They don't seem to grasp this concept. They continue to do what they've always done, namely snapping out orders, demanding unquestioned obedience, protecting their child from taking responsibility for their own actions and controlling everything their child does, thinks or touches.

The child's cell phone serves as the world's longest umbilical cord.

Hover parents assume the same parenting style that worked for very young children will work for teenagers.

Crazed with parental power, they laugh maniacally, like a James Bond villain, but now their subjects don't quiver and obey like they used to. Instead, they just reattach their ear buds and continue texting.

When our kids hit the teenage years, my Beloved and I read books to make sense of it. We knew we needed to change, but weren't smart enough to figure out how to wend our way through this uncharted territory without a map.

Sex Education

With three kids only two years apart (a boy and identical twin girls), we hit adolescence like a bug splats on a windshield. Add an equally unstable, pre-menopausal wife to the mix and my Beloved longed to take up residence in a Motel 6.

I latched on to a great little volume targeting girls ages 9 to 15 titled *What's Happening to My Body?* It was the Forward by author Linda Madaras that saved me. She talked about how parents are always terrified their daughters will have sex and get pregnant, when in reality a preteen girl just wants to know what the haddie-daddle is going on in there.

Instead of using the time-honored tradition of pitching a book in a young girl's room with a terse "Read this and ask if you have any questions" the author recommended actually sitting down together to peruse the book, no matter how embarrassed the mother might be.

Employing this sage wisdom, my twin daughters and I arranged ourselves comfortably on the sofa, a daughter on either side of me, and commenced reading.

I was shocked to discover there are five stages of breast development.

Following an intensive group inspection, we decided Twin A was a Stage 2 with Twin B running a close second in Stage 1½. I silently wondered if my little lentils would ever attain Stage 5.

The best interaction while reading this book together was when the girls discovered their very own mom had already been through this puzzling process (who knew?) and now her job was to hold their hands and lead them out of the dark forest of girlhood down the rutted road of adolescence into the sunny meadow of womanhood.

Mom was not their sworn enemy; she was their most dependable friend. Light bulbs flashed. Cat claws retracted.

The tone of our conversations changed too. Modeling Ms. Madaras' communication suggestions, I learned to craft choices characterized as the "Childish Option" or the more desirable "Grown-up Option."

I was growing up right alongside the girls and it felt great!

Ms. Madaras wrote a similar treatise targeting boys and dads, but my Beloved scoffed at the prospect of such a new-fangled concept and opted instead to let our son learn about sex the right way – from his peers during junior high gym class.

Laundry

I discovered another life-changing volume titled *Raising Self-Reliant Children in a Self-Indulgent World*. Authors Stephen

Glenn and Jane Nelsen, a husband/wife psychologist team, parented 17 kids, some birthed, some adopted, more fostered. That's some serious parenting qualifications. Or an express ticket to the loony bin.

Anyway, Glenn and Jane said the job of parents is to produce individuals who by the age of eighteen can take care of themselves, their possessions, their finances, their jobs and their relationships.

They also stressed that as an adult, these individuals must be able to plan, shop for, COOK, eat and clean up a complete balanced meal that did not originate from a drive-in window.

What a surprise! So that's the whole parenting job description.

Thus empowered, we set to work industriously passing off chores to our teenagers who welcomed this next step into adulthood as if it were toe fungus.

The first task we handed over was laundry. Painstakingly I instructed the assembled multitude on the mechanics of sorting colors and whites, the respective properties of hot and cold water, and all appropriate washing machine and dryer settings.

I spoke lovingly of laundry soap and fabric softener, of proper folding techniques and the fresh smell of clean sheets on your bed. We practiced together. We all agreed that this was indeed a Major Step toward Maturity.

Then I turned the task over to them and stepped back to watch.

Right off the bat we hit a little snag – in spite of all my training we still maintained wildly different perceptions of what "doing the laundry" actually meant.

Parents, in their tedious and ancient brains, think "doing the laundry" consists of seven distinct steps:

1. Place soiled garments in the dirty clothes basket daily.

2. Once a week carry the basket to the laundry room.

3. Sort the garments by color and temperature settings.

4. Load soiled garments into the washing machine, select the correct temperature, add soap, and press START.

5. Place wet items in the dryer, select the correct temperature and press START.

6. Neatly fold all clean garments, stacking them in orderly piles in the laundry basket.

7. Return the laundry basket of orderly stacks to your room and place them in their proper storage places.

Teenagers' perceptions of "doing laundry" include only steps 4 and 5 above. They express no concern whatsoever for the condition or location of the garments both pre and post washing.

Sloth

Additionally, although you spent those halcyon years of childhood teaching them how to put away their all toys and make up their beds, these skills vanish overnight and are replaced by slothful habits that would make a barnyard animal proud.

They take to randomly flinging items off their bodies immediately upon entering the house, quickly turning it into a hoarder's paradise.

My Beloved instituted Pop's Store with inventory gleaned from all the kids' stuff he collected each evening. The next morning they had to re-purchase important necessities such as underwear, shin guards, sport uniforms, dance costumes, assorted shoes, school books and band instruments.

This teaching strategy, though painful, effectively penetrated their mysterious teenage brains and the house returned to its previous less cluttered state.

But now a new problem cropped up. All their junk now resided in a two foot deep thatch on the floor of their rooms. The main reason it was two feet deep was because they didn't own any more stuff to throw down there. Here's the difficult lesson of assigning teenagers duties: the delegator suffers more than the delegatee.

As you pass by their open doorways, your mind conjures up many troubling thoughts:

"OMG just look at the mess in there. How can they ever find anything clean to wear? OMG what if they wear dirty clothes to school? OMG they'll smell bad, look worse and the teacher won't like them. If the teacher doesn't like them, they won't pass. If they don't pass junior high, they won't get to high school. If they don't pass high school, they'll never get into college. If they don't go to college, they'll have to settle for a job flipping burgers and it won't be enough to support them so they'll have to take up robbing 7-Elevens to make ends meet. Next thing you know, they'll become professional burglars stealing TVs, cell phones and hubcaps. Then they'll open a chop shop to rub ID numbers off car batteries and most likely they'll end up in jail for the rest of their lives."

All this miasma of misery in the scant 0.00013 seconds it takes to glance into their disgusting rooms. You begin shielding your eyes from the sight to control your rising alarm.

More importantly, you realized you really don't care if your children wear dirty clothes to school. You just fear the humiliation of the teacher gossiping that you're not a "good mother."

No matter how hard you try to prepare your little hatchlings for the Practical Things of Life, stuff happens.

You sneer at stories of hover mothers sending their boys off to college, young men who have never lifted a finger around the house turning their tidy whiteys pink with the first load of laundry. Not your children, you vow. No siree.

Instead your little rocket scientist, although responsible for his own laundry for the better part of six years, arrives at university unfamiliar with the concept of not-in-home washing facilities, i.e. laundromats, and thus can't figure out how to put coins in the machines.

The good news is that the college freshman who formerly stockpiled his garments on the floor of his room, returns home at Thanksgiving break to announce his miraculous discovery that you can actually store dirty clothes IN THE LAUNDRY BASKET!!!

Driving

Of course, teenagers provide much more advanced suffering opportunities for all parents, not just hovering mommies and daddies.

This is the part of parenthood that's so confusing because you're constantly tip toeing through the shards of broken glass, trying to help them learn important life lessons without killing themselves.

And there are so many pitfalls – dating, driving, drinking, dating while driving, dating while drinking, driving while drinking, driving while dating and drinking, and most dangerous of all, driving while texting.

Scratch the parent of a fifteen year old, soon to be sixteen and of drivable age, and you will find a mommy terrified for her child's safety and freedom, and a father calculating the cost of buying a car and insuring a teen driver.

Insurance companies invest in giant supercomputers capable of determining the distance to far off galaxies or how many miscellaneous molecules it takes to compose a substance that can be packaged and sold as a "chicken nugget." But even these high-powered processors can't calculate the actual cost of insuring a male teenage driver.

However, check in with these same frightened parents six months later when their oldest child now eagerly fetches his younger sister from ballet, drives her to soccer, then dashes to the grocery store for milk and sprouts, careens back to the soccer field to collect her, then on to piano lessons, then the dry cleaners, back to the piano studio before finally steering for home.

Ask that parent about their former fears and they laugh in your face. They can't even remember how they survived before their oldest could drive.

And that's the thing about raising kids.

They're not toddlers forever. Most of them eventually get potty trained and learn to put their clothes on frontwards because these skills are key elements for lifelong success.

Likewise, they're not teenagers forever either. Many of them collect a series of related facts from various educational institutions and occasionally graduate. Most adult children sooner or later move out of your house and go on to become productive citizens – if you let them.

And learning how to laugh is a lifesaver.

It's the hover parents – the ones who cling to their children's coat tails for dear life, nagging them to do their homework and take their chewable vitamins, still fighting their battles and making excuses for them and forever blaming any other human being who dares to make life "hard" for their child – that never seem to grow up.

Relax, oh you who hover. Children are a fantastic source of joy and laughter for several reasons.

1. They do funny things.

2. They don't realize they do funny things.

3. If they're teenagers, they do incredibly stupid things.

4. Also when they're teenagers and you're laughing about them, they're never around to defend themselves.

Long ago one of my four-year-olds announced she wanted "to be a fire engine" when she grew up. Much later, as a grown up college student, this individual rediscovered the quote and remarked, "Mom, that doesn't make any sense."

That's when I discovered humor is a high-level thinking skill and we weren't there yet.

Laughter is how we express and expunge anxiety. And goodness knows there's more than ample anxiety in birthing, raising and launching people out into the world.

Laughing about the tough stuff keeps you healthy, happy and sane.

Harmful Parenting Assumptions

ASSSUMPTION #1: I can control my child's environment.

Yes you can, as long as your child is constantly within your sight. That time ends with his or her entry into nursery school. But the deeper question to ponder is WHY?

It's not good to insulate children from the world, to fight their battles and make their excuses. That's just your paranoia and fear that you might experience horrible pain if something bad actually happened to them.

ASSUMPTION #2: My child is better off staying in my safe protective bubble.

Not really. Albert Einstein said, "The most important decision we will ever make is whether we believe the universe is friendly or unfriendly."

People who believe the universe is unfriendly are defensive, fearful and overly protective. Parents who believe the universe is friendly have a much better chance of nurturing their children to make healthy and wise choices.

ASSUMPTION #3: My child is my property.

Hmmm, just like your wife or your husband is your property? We're talking about a human life here, not slavery.

God has entrusted you with the responsibility of guiding and nurturing a tiny human being into adulthood. That means raising a person who is physically, mentally, emotionally and spiritually mature and healthy. Hovering harms this development.

ASSUMPTION #4: My teenager is an adversary that must be controlled.

Really? And I bet you have problems getting along with people at work, too. You're intimidated and frightened by the loss of the parental power club you used to wield over your child's head.

As your child moves closer to maturity, you need to sharpen your adaptability skills. Parenting is a journey from omnipotence over a two-year-old to equality with an adult.

ASSUMPTION #5: My child will be successful in the way I want him to be.

That one works great in patriarchal cultures which also embrace the parent's right to kill their children as punishment for disobedience, but not so much in modern societies.

Most children really want to please their parents, or at least not incur their wrath. The hover parent demands slavish OBEDIENCE from their offspring. A more productive approach is to help the child discover and maximize his talents.

Healthy Parenting Actions

ACTION #1: Focus on the product you're producing – a relatively happy taxpaying adult.

Keeping your eye on the horizon helps you rise above the ebb and flow of daily frustrations. Children learn their coping skills from watching you. You're teaching your child how to craft a life full of love, joy, peace, patience, kindness, goodness, gentleness, faithfulness, and self-control. You need to model those same gifts. It helps to read good parenting books and also to pray.

ACTION #2: Control your fears, not your child.

As I hope you've figured out from laughing about it that you can't exercise absolute control over another human being, even if they are unfortunate enough to be your child. Confront what you fear most which is probably the pain of losing him or her.

It's true that awful things can happen to your baby. But most of the time they don't. And worrying yourself sick isn't going to change the outcome.

Stop trying to manipulate your child's life and get a grip. Prepare your child to go out into the world with your blessing.

ACTION #3: Know when to push and when to pull your child.

Children are immature and need your guidance. But they also need your patience, forgiveness, and shared joy. Be wise enough to gently let go.

As a school board member I attended 43 graduation ceremonies over the course of nine years. The saddest one – the one I'll never forget – was when the Valedictorian's father did not allow him to attend because he (the father) thought it was more important for him (the son) to stay home and study.

Hover parents beware.

ACTION #4: Laugh about the tough stuff.

Laughter will heal the fears, blunders and mistakes you're going to make.

The sooner YOU laugh, the faster your relationship with your child will heal.

If you laugh enough, you'll discover it's even more fun being a parent than it was being a child.

Parenting is a joyful, exhilarating, rewarding, and exhausting experience. And when they're grown up, you can take a nap.

Lighten up and grow up
with your children

I'd Rather Die Than Speak in Public! Really?

"According to most studies, people's number one fear is public speaking. Number two is death. This means to the average person, if you go to a funeral, you're better off in the casket than doing the eulogy."
Jerry Seinfeld

Do you have a vision of what you want to be when you grow up? I wanted to be Audrey Hepburn.

Mainly I wanted to look sophisticated like Audrey in her *Breakfast at Tiffany's* little black dress, swan-like neck and pearls.

Of course, I didn't want to do any hard work or step outside of my comfort zone to be like her. I just wanted my fairy godmother to wave a magic wand, and violá I would be "discovered" and effortlessly elevated to star and wear beautiful clothes and just generally be adored.

Yeah, right.

My first step to stardom was staring in the first grade play as Goldilocks, my cute bouncy Shirley Temple curls carefully secured with a barrette and ribbons.

While Jimmy Doyle barfed backstage (and he was only playing a tree for god's sake) I soared to magical heights out in front of the footlights.

I distinctly remember standing stage left (or was it stage right – I still can't keep them straight) looking out at the assembled multitude and thinking "this is where I belong."

But as it turned out, the stage was not where I belonged, mainly because I didn't want to work for it.

Oh, there were more shows in high school and college, but when it came time to quit hiding in academia and actually take a chance in the "real world" by going to New York, I didn't have the courage and sheer guts it takes to pursue my dreams.

Because they weren't really goals; they were just wishful thinking.

So I took the safe, easy route and went into business mainly because the telephone company where I'd been working as a long distance operator plopped a managerial job in my lap.

As Suzanne Evans says, "the way you do anything is the way you do everything." I always took the easy way out, never venturing outside the ordinary.

Any of you do that? Sure you do. At one time or another we've all taken the easy way out.

I wasn't original enough or good enough or competitive enough to expend any effort on making the performing wish come true. So I hunkered down in the safe worlds of business, marriage, kids, pets and PTA.

Go for Your Dream

Then one morning 30 years later I woke up and decided I wanted to be a professional speaker when I grew up.

The difference between being a speaker and an actor is – a speaker has to make up their own lines. And this time, instead of wishful thinking, I actually began working on it.

I was 50 years old. Our son was in college and our twin daughters were juniors in high school. I figured it was time for me to get a life.

I spent the next 18 months thinking up something to say that people might want to listen to – AND pay money to hear.

I thought I was a pretty good speaker because:

a. My smashing debut as Goldilocks had put stars in my eyes, AND
b. I'd taught several business classes and no one complained about my talks or actually walked out, SO
c. I must be good.

Someone invited me to a Toastmasters Club meeting and I sauntered in quite full of myself, ready to show these people how it's really done.

Okay, so let me just say here that Toastmasters is an 80+ year old international organization that helps people improve their platform and leadership skills.

In order to make you aware of your unconscious mannerisms, they honk a horn or tap a bell every time you say "um" or "ah" or fiddle with your hair or clasp your hands or pick your nose or whatever it is your body instinctively does when it's nervous.

This system is VERY effective and has helped literally millions of people overcome their fears and obstacles to success.

When it came time for me to give my first speech, I strode confidently to the front of the room and commenced talking about my favorite subject – ME.

Like many people who imagine their presentation is excellent simply because no one throws rotten tomatoes, I thought I had knocked it out of the park – until I received the constructive feedback from my evaluator.

Bless his heart, Tom Corbin carefully counted all 43 "um's" and "ah's" in my scant six minute speech. That's 7.2 "um's" per minute – an international indoor world record!

I was shocked – and disgraced, but good news, it got my attention that I wasn't nearly as spectacular as I thought I was.

Lesson learned: just because people don't complain to your face doesn't mean you're an effective presenter. If you don't connect, they won't tell you. They just won't hire you, won't accept your ideas or won't buy your stuff.

I love to laugh about this humbling failure now because it was exactly the kick in the booty that I needed to get my attention. Otherwise I might have gone sailing out the door still thinking I was God's gift to the communication world.

How do you react when you receive criticism? Do you get defensive and fight back or accept it and work to improve?

Well, I took it as a sign that the emperor (me) wore no clothes and if I wanted to pursue my dreams, I'd better work on how I presented myself to the public.

Work on How You Talk

Have you ever noticed that when you buy a new car, all of a sudden you see a million of the same model driving around when before you'd never noticed them?

That's how it was with "um's" and "ah's." Every time I opened my mouth, a torrent of unnecessary and annoying filler words tumbled out. My favorites fillers to this day are "so" or for a complete change of pace "and so."

If you're a twenty-something then you're probably addicted to "you know," "like" and "awesome" as in "Dude, like you know that was so you know like awesome!" Eliminating these crutch words may leave you totally tongue-tied. Give it a try. I dare you.

Now you might think filler words are a trivial preoccupation, but you would be wrong.

Listen to the attractive (and well paid) people on sports broadcasts and talk shows – unscripted situations – and the most illustrious personalities will have virtually no "um's" "ah's" or "likes."

These successful folks are able to string together a series of sentences containing complete thoughts without pausing, stammering or groping for words.

Of course, these "thoughts" are not necessarily DEEP in the sense of making a difference to mankind. They're mainly banal chitchat about ball scores and RBI's and first downs and defensive versus offensive plays and giving 110%, like that's possible.

But the speakers care passionately about these issues and can go on for hours, especially if there was pass interference. They **sound** intelligent and profound unless you stop to listen to what they're actually saying.

Now flip to Jerry Springer. In between all the yelling, screaming, cursing, chair throwing and lunging to whup each other, it's hard to grasp even an occasional word of English.

The Springer folks may all be filthy rich just like the sports commentators, but I doubt it.

Not only do they sound like idiots, but they LOOK like bozos as well, what with the head to toe tattoos and wife-beater t-shirts barely covering their enormous beer bellies. You would not want to invite these tacky people over for dinner.

Why?

Because everything about them communicates: "My life is out of control and I am an uncivilized moron!"

Here's the point: Everything about you communicates something. The way you look. The way you talk. The way you act. The way you react. You cannot NOT communicate what you are.

People who want to be successful start by looking and sounding successful.

Anyway, my observation is that how you talk matters. The more smoothly and fluently you are able to compose and roll out your thoughts, the more money you will make. It's that simple.

Your accent matters too. Interestingly, most people for whom English is their second language work hard to speak clearly and be understood. Conversely, native born English speakers rarely work to improve their pronunciation.

Although I grew up in Texas, my parents were refugees from North Carolina where everyone knows your great granddaddy and all decent civilization ends west of the Smokey Mountains.

Mom spoke with a dulcet southern drawl. For example, even after 60 years in the hinterlands of the Lone Star state, she still hadn't mastered the word "porch." It came out with three syllables and no "r". "Po-wa-ch."

Thus, my accent sounded like a cross between Scarlet O'Hara ("Uh do da-cla-ya, Rhett!") and President Lyndon Johnson ("Maw feller Mer-kins"). For those of you too young to have ever heard him, Lyndon possessed a Texas twang so dense it was like driving a Mack truck through the Alamo.

In college I wanted to try out for a Shakespearian production, but the director told me he couldn't cast me until I lost the accent. You just can't do Shakespeare sounding like Larry the Cable Guy.

"Romeo, Romeo, wh-e –aw fo aught th-eo-ow, Romeo?"

So I sat in a tiny closet (the school called it a studio) with a reel-to-reel tape recorder and listened to myself massacre the English language until I finally learned how to speak accent-free.

This experience was the single most valuable skill I learned in my four years of higher education – with the possible exception of the discovery that if you're crawling through a barbed wire fence in the middle of the night, imbedding the pointy things in your face results in permanent scars.

Since I could now articulate fairly clearly, I set to work trying to corral my stumbling, mumbling, bumbling speech patterns. It was hard, but I persisted.

Next I turned my attention to my looks.

Reinvent Your Look

Let me just say – they needed work.

Over the course of centuries (20th and 21st) I'd packed on a couple of extra pounds – 40 to be exact, which would be perfect – if I was just nine inches taller.

To compensate, I'd adopted a quasi-maternity fashion statement specializing in baggy, tent-like couture with just a hint of whimsical orthotics.

Menopause had not been kind to me. In fact, it had whacked me with the ugly stick complete with laugh lines, prune lips and abundant chin hairs. In summary, I was one hot mess.

First I had to develop a vision of what I wanted to become. I gave up trying to look like Audrey Hepburn. I realized that no matter how charming a little black dress (LBD) I might acquire, it would still house a chubby body topped with my crinkled face.

Plus, part of my gift to the Keep America Beautiful campaign was never to appear in public with my flabby bat wings exposed, even though the Second Amendment clearly guarantees us the right to bear arms.

In other words, my ideal LBD could best be described in one word – burka.

Okay, so maybe I'd let myself go. It really helps to assess the damages of time and reinvent yourself every so often.

How I wish it was as easy to lose weight as it is to lose the car keys, your cell phone, your temper or your mind. My body and my fat were such good friends that they really fought to stay together.

Obesity is a mental state of mind brought on by boredom and disappointment. It's not about WHAT you eat, but about WHO you are when you eat it.

It was time to start an intensive self-improvement regimen, to release the thinner, more attractive and successful person hiding inside my frumpy middle-aged body.

Sadly, dieting isn't a piece of cake. For starters I gave up M&Ms and snicker doodles, and then considered using super glue for lip gloss. Slowly, reluctantly, tediously I quit treating the temple of my body like a drive-through.

Over the course of my lifetime I've probably lost about 137 pounds, but they always come back and find me.

Exercise for Fun and Profit

However, the dream of becoming stage-worthy called for even more drastic measures than just limiting intake. I was going to have to exercise. Holy Yuck!

I've never enjoyed working out. My idea of exercise is a good, brisk sit.

It's hard to make time for something you hate. I argued that I didn't have time for exercise.

But oddly I did have time to watch TV cooking shows like Celebrity Turkey Basting, grocery shop for exotic ingredients, cook for hours on a recipe that claimed a 30 minute prep time, serve it to the family and then decline to eat because it wasn't "on my diet."

At length and at last however, I finally showed up at a gym. The thing about Americans and working out is that at the gym you strain really hard to break a sweat, while never actually accomplishing anything remotely productive – like picking cotton or scrubbing toilets.

The first day a very nice trainer named Joan, a former Olympian, showed me how to use several machines. As I emphatically insisted that I wanted to "feel the burn" she quizzically cocked her head to ask "Does your back ever hurt?"

"Yes, of course. Doesn't everybody's? Why?"

"Well, you're all crooked and twisted so you shouldn't work with weights until you fix it because you'll just do it wrong."

She took me over to a padded bench and instructed me to "lie down." That sounded fine to me – exercising by lying down.

It turned out that I didn't know how to lie down properly. I don't mean the act of lying down. I mean simply resting on a surface in a reclining position. How could I be 50+ years old and not have mastered the skill of lying prone?

Thus began my advanced training in the art of proper lounging. I'm not making this up. After a couple of weeks of intense practice I finally graduated to sitting and finally to walking.

Surprisingly, my back began to feel better and after a while, she permitted me to start working on machines with weights.

The thing about weights is they were invented for the sole purpose of – follow me closely here – being heavy. That's it. They are without doubt the most useless invention in the history of humankind.

But there you are at the gym for Pete's sake with all these perspiring people laboring to hoist them up as if the fate of the world depended upon defying gravity. So I too began heaving and pumping iron.

Many gyms offer even more unusual forms of useless movement than just weight lifting. These exercises come in the form of *aerobics* which is a fancy word for jumping up and down. Or *yoga* where you strike exotic poses. Or *spinning* where you ride a bike to nowhere pedaling so hard you puke.

Then there's Zumba. The word Zumba is derived from the Greek, "zum" meaning "very fast" and "ba" meaning "like sheep."

You assemble in a room with a bunch of other overweight people where a sadistic drill sergeant turns up the music so loud blood runs from your ears. Then she starts shouting instructions and bouncing around while you desperately try to imitate all the weird motions she's making.

Zumba is the worst dance class ever. Imagine a room of Republicans doing hip-hop, soca, samba, salsa, merengue, mambo and martial arts all together and doing it badly, even for Republicans. That's Zumba. Personally, I would avoid it.

Over time and with determined effort my body reluctantly parted with several pounds of flab.

I'd also developed enough inner confidence so in the words of the song from *West Side Story* that Maria sang just before her lover stabbed her brother to death, "I Feel Pretty."

Develop Your Unique Style

You have no idea how hard it is for a short frumpy middle aged woman to look casually contemporary, mature yet trendy, age-appropriate but not matronly, old but still relevant, glamorous yet approachable, modestly plump yet fit, in short – to look like an Authentic Fake.

I enlisted the aid of my Fashion Police daughter who took me shopping. We arrived at Ann Taylor, a store that caters to young career types and from which she had purchased many charming ensembles.

I tried on a pair of peg-leg pants so tight I looked like I'd been poured into them but forgot to say "when" because my muffin tops spilled over the sides.

Apparently you have to have an hourglass figure to be an Ann Taylor woman. Unfortunately my waist had long since disappeared when one year I gave it up for Lent.

Next we tried a waist-free, blimp-oriented garment store, but that sent me back to the aforementioned tent-awning look. Another establishment offered clothing simply perfect for the glamorous woman shuffling behind a walker.

Eventually I discovered Chico's, a store that caters to the full-bodied but still fashion-functioning older woman. Since that time, and not coincidentally, my store has doubled in size. They really should have the common decency to name the new wing after me.

Time passed. I finally conquered my speaking woes, learned how to dress myself, got passionate about the topic of laughing at foolish human assumptions, and set out on my journey to stardom through motivational speaking.

For those of you who think speaking is a glamorous business (and maybe in the beginning I did too) let me just say that you only spend about 5% of your time actually holding a microphone.

The other 95% is spent studying, reading, traveling, retrieving lost luggage, writing proposals, updating your website, writing your blog and newsletter, and begging people for the opportunity to stand up in front of their folks and blab.

But I'm not complaining. I love it and at last am doing the work I was put on this earth to do – namely offering hope to people by inspiring, engaging, and entertaining them.

I've also learned that one of the best ways to lose weight and get healthy is purposeful living. Sitting around directionless is a perfect recipe for broadening your butt, not your horizons.

Now I realize most sane people don't aspire to a career in professional speaking, but my point here is that EVERYONE presents themselves to the world every day and in every interaction with another human being.

The more polished your image, the MORE MONEY you make.

Create Your Personal Brand

It never ceases to amaze me that intelligent, business-savvy people, as part of their job, stand up and present their ideas and products with the confidence and expertise of celery.

They fail to recognize that public speaking is an acquired skill that improves with practice and honest feedback. Speaking effectively for 20 minutes before the right group of people can do more for your career than spending a year behind a desk!

But, effective presenting is not just about how you look and talk. It's also about WHAT you say.

You are presenting yourself as a brand. What value do you bring to the organization? The situation? The problem at hand? To the audience sitting before you? What is your unique contribution to making the world a better place?

One of my coaching clients, we'll call her Rhonda, asked me to help her prepare a ten minute presentation to the partners in her firm. Based upon this talk they would decide whether to offer her a partnership. Clearly this speech contained huge make it or break it risks and rewards.

Initially, I think Rhonda just wanted help organizing her PowerPoint slides and maybe tightening her opening and conclusion. Fifteen minutes into our consultation it was evident that she needed to re-think the entire approach of her speech.

You see, Rhonda planned to talk about her historical accomplishments as a long-time manger at the firm, citing various projects she'd completed on time and under budget. But a partner position requires more than being an efficient order taker. It requires leadership.

Rhonda redesigned her entire program to talk about how she could and would help the company grow in quality and client service. In other words, she established her value not just as a reliable foot soldier, but also as a leader and visionary in moving the firm forward to greater growth and profitability.

At the conclusion of our coaching sessions, Rhonda having accepted herself as a leader worthy of becoming partner said and I quote, "I'm ready to step into my eminence."

WOW! What a powerful phrase!!

Are you ready to step into your eminence?

How do you present yourself to the world every day? Do you appear intelligent, confident, competent, clean?

Or are you just one step removed from Springer folk?

Do you ever wonder what some people are thinking as they get dressed in the morning?

In this day and age of "finding yourself" and "being anything you want to be" and wearing your "underwear' on the outside of your clothes, a lot of people are making their lives a lot harder than they really need to be.

Take for example the millennial who shows up for a job interview dressed in shorts and flip-flops. You may think I'm kidding here, but this is a major corporate complaint today about twenty-somethings.

Just because Mark Zuckerberg gets away with a hoodie and exposed hairy toes doesn't mean employers are OK with you dressing down for an interview.

Or consider the young hottie whose business attire closely approximates silk lingerie.

Speaking of the bedroom, there's actually a product called "Bed Head" wherein for only $24.95 you can transform your disheveled hair from the way it looks when you first wake up in the morning into a stylish mess that looks even worse.

Oscar Wilde said "Be yourself. Everyone else is taken." Sadly, some people really should realize that 'being themselves" is not all that charming.

Many individuals spend enormous amounts of time, energy and money on decorating their outer body with fancy clothes, hair and makeup, but pay absolutely no attention to how they sound and what value they bring to an organization.

Donald Trump
Angelina Jolie
Mike Tyson
Paris Hilton
Justin Bieber
Ellen DeGeneres

All these people have a distinctive personal brand – not necessarily good, but very distinctive.

Some are these people are fools, some are divas, all are (or were at one time) wealthy, but the point is – each one of them communicates with YOU – generating a gut reaction at the mere mention of their name.

That, my friends, is the power of brand and presence.

Think of yourself as a brand. Are you a competent business person tricked out like a street punk? Or are you the body of Rosie O'Donnell with the brains of Britney Spears?

You may not be famous, but you have some effect on everyone you meet. The question is – does your presence work FOR or AGAINST you?

Positive Presence occurs when you are perceived as totally focused on the matter at hand *and* on being of value to *the other person.*

Negative Presence conveys the feeling that you are maneuvering or manipulating the person or situation for your own self-serving ambition or agenda.

When you are totally present with another person, people spontaneously trust, have confidence in and respect you.

If you're planning a bright tomorrow and you haven't started branding yourself with positive presence, what are you waiting for? Yesterday?

Think of Bill Gates of Microsoft or Jack Canfield of Chicken Soup fame. What have they got that you don't have? Oh yeah, billions of dollars – but they also have a kick-ass personal brand.

A personal brand isn't about how great you think you are. It's about the value you bring to others. Jack Canfield's value is the hope and integrity his books bring to readers.

Without regard for whether you are an Apple or a PC aficionado, Bill Gates' vision of personal computers changed the world forever. Now he and wife Melinda are using their vast wealth to bring birth control and freedom from malaria to folks living in third world countries.

Then there are people who have risen from extreme poverty to become symbols of cultural opportunity simply by improving their personal presence so people could see the talent inside.

James Earl Jones was born and raised in Arkabutla, Mississippi but how far would his career have progressed if he continued to talk like Buckwheat?

All these examples are people who took the time to learn to create a brand and a positive presence. Every one of them had to overcome numerous challenges to become successful.

Bottom line: you can't have style if you don't have substance.

It is **easy to be excellent** these days because so many people are choosing to be mediocre.

So get to work on releasing the fabulously successful person trapped inside you!

Personal Presence Assumptions

ASSUMPTION #1: People just need to accept me the way I am.

Yes, AND that kind of thinking will guarantee you an exciting career in which the phrase "Would you like fries with that?" figures prominently.

Whether you agree or not people are going to make judgments about you – actually within the first 7 to 10 seconds after they lay eyes on you. It's human nature.

Why create an uphill battle for yourself you by looking low class, immature, self-absorbed, lazy, and incompetent?

ASSUMPTION #2: I'm afraid to speak, so I'll just ignore it until I step to the microphone.

It's crazy that many people in leadership roles requiring public speaking refuse to practice and refine this skill. No wait, they do practice – they just do it in front of the live audience.

Ineffective executives in top positions are especially guilty of reading speeches to their employees. Hello, McFly! These people work for you. You're paying them to sit there and listen to you drone on. Nobody's going to tell the Emperor s/he's a loser.

You're probably thinking: I'm afraid someone may criticize me and tell me I'm not good at speaking so I'll just step to the microphone and muddle through.

Is this logical? Not hardly.

It's like a race car driver saying, "I might have an accident going that fast so I'll just practice during the race."

What could possibly go wrong with this plan?

Well, the race car driver endangers the lives of all the other drivers. And the unpracticed speaker insults and bores everyone in the audience by stumbling through his/her comments.

ASSUMPTION #3: Why prepare? I'll just wing it when I get up there.

The people in the audience are giving you the gift of their time. Please don't waste this valuable commodity.

Besides, trying to compose your thoughts impromptu means your remarks are most surely going to be less than dynamic.

Abraham Lincoln famously said "Better to remain silent and be thought a fool than to speak and remove all doubt."

Preparation will make you less likely to reveal your inner fool.

ASSUMPTION #4: I spek gooder den udder peeps.

Sure you do, based upon what empirical evidence? Your friends and family? They all spek jest like you.

If you want to achieve more success, then striving to master a more universal grasp of the language is a wise investment of time and energy.

To quote Steve Martin "Some people have a way with words. Others not have way."

Words properly used are a compelling sign of intelligence and aptitude. Used improperly, they are a death knell to upward mobility.

ASSUMPTION #5: English is my native language so I don't need no practice.

There are a jillion ways to speak English. Successful people learn to marginalize the damage of their regional or ethnic accents.

People in other countries watch American TV to learn English. Observe closely and you'll discover that actors in sitcoms use hick sounding accents for their characters to add humor or, frankly, to make them appear lazy and stupid.

It doesn't matter whether the accent is a Southern drawl, Texas twang, California valley girl or surfer dude, Cajun jumble, Jersey snarl, African American ghetto or Hispanic street smart – it makes the speaker sound less intelligent.

The absolute best way to fast-track your career is learning to enunciate properly when necessary. You can always fall back into street vernacular with your homeys.

ASSUMPTION #6: I'm an expert on my topic so I'm prepared enough.

Of course you know your topic; that goes without saying. That's the minimum required to stand up at the microphone.

The problem is that many speakers waste the precious first five minutes inanely commenting on the weather or rattling change in their pockets trying to kick-start their limpid brains.

Once they finally get into their expertise they're pretty competent. They problem is that while they were groping around trying to get focused most of the listeners left the room.

I don't mean they physically walked out. I mean they tuned you out. Your competition is NOT other speakers. It's cell phones, iPads and all their many apps which are waaay more interesting than your faltering, irrelevant, inane opening comments.

ASSUMPTION #7: My PowerPoint presentation will tell it all.

"Death by PowerPoint" means subjecting your unfortunate audience members to insanely boring presentation hell.

If your PP is going to tell the whole story, then there's no need for YOU. Save time and just email it to everybody.

By seeking safety behind the bulwark of the lectern, you become a barely visible tiny talking head. Now compound the error by standing in the dark because you turned the lights down so everybody can see your tedious slides. This is the sure sign of a rank amateur.

Do us all a favor and just phone in your presentation.

Great sheet music doesn't make a great musician. You have to know how to play it.

ASSUMPTION #8: The sky will fall if I make a mistake.

No it won't. You're just allowing your fear of failure to take control. Trust me on this one. All kinds of goofy things have happened to me mid-speech and the world is still in its celestial orbit.

True story – I'm on a stage in front of about 200 people, hot into my topic, enthusiastically pacing back and forth, when BLAM – suddenly I'm lying flat on my back. It occurs so unexpectedly I can't quite figure out what happened.

As I crawl around retrieving the microphone and the PP clicker, then clambering ungracefully to my feet, the audience of primarily very nice school teachers watches dispassionately.

Finally I figure it out. I have just FALLEN OFF MY SHOES!

Apparently there's a knack to not tipping over on platform sandals which clearly I had not yet mastered.

It must have been a spectacular fall – very Jim Carey cartoon-like with feet, legs and arms flying in all directions. I really wish I could have seen it.

Meanwhile, the ladies continued silently watching.

My speech was all about the benefits of laughing about the tough stuff of life as soon as possible. I figured this was a grand opportunity to practice what I preach.

As I sought to re-attach the lavaliere microphone, rearrange my undergarments and just generally reassemble my discombobulated self I made several funny remarks about what just happened.

At that point the entire group of very compassionate ladies rose up as one giant mass of overly concerned femininity. "Are you OK?!!?!" they exclaimed. "We thought it was part of your act! We were waiting to see what would happen next."

People won't notice if you make a mistake.

Here's another corker.

I was teaching in a basement classroom when I felt something touch my hair, but being a professional I continued on. The students all sat there stone faced.

A few minutes later I felt a tickle on my scalp. Now I'm a Texas girl so naturally I sport big hair, heavily back-combed and held in place with a quart of shellac-like hair spray, so there's plenty of air space in my coif.

There it was again, only the tickle seemed to have moved. Still total silence from the audience. A third tickle...

At last I paused and reached up to scratch the irritation when YEEEEEEEECK I discovered a ROACH nesting in my tresses!!!!!

I've experienced some disgusting things in life, but having a roach in your hair is right at the top of my list. It's even grosser than baby poop under your fingernails.

I screamed, frantically brushed my head, dislodged several unglued strands of hair and also the roach which promptly flew off to continuing doing whatever roaches do.

As I stood there quaking I implored the group "Why didn't you tell me?" They responded "We just wanted to see what would happen."

Now if I didn't die from the embarrassment of having a roach jump into my hair, then believe me the world is not going to stop turning if you make a little mistake at the microphone.

So get over yourself and get out there. Conquer your fear of public speaking and present the best possible you to the world.

Personal Presence Improvement Actions

ACTION #1: Make a realistic assessment of how you look and sound.

Studies show that having money and being good looking don't make you happy. However, neither does being broke and ugly, so get to work on yourself.

Video tape AND make a separate audio recording of yourself giving a short 5-7 minute speech. Use your cell phone. It doesn't have to be formal or even in front of actual live victims. You can do it in the privacy of your own home.

The camera and the microphone will magnify your limitations. Now you absolutely positively must WATCH IT. It does no good to make the recording and be too scared to view it.

Believe me when I say that watching yourself on film can be horrifying. Turn a critical eye to your appearance.

- Are you dressed appropriately for the occasion? Rule of thumb is that you should dress one level higher than your audience is dressed. It gives you unspoken authority.

- Do your clothes fit or do they need alterations? Are your clothes the right size for your current body proportions or are the buttons straining to contain your excess belly?

- You think your hair looks fabulous from the front, but what about from the side and back? Is your hairdo appropriate?

- Are you standing up straight or slouching? Do you look purposeful and confident or timid and scared?

- Are you flaunting your ethnicity, gender preference or style of dress? Daring your audience to take offense at your over-the-top choices will hold you back when you're trying to up-level.

No matter how smooth and intelligent and powerful you may think you are, it is always humbling to see yourself as others see you – unless of course you're a complete narcissist.

Now locate someone who is successfully doing the kind of work you aspire to and ask them to watch, listen and critique. Pay close attention to what they say and DON'T ARGUE or DEFEND yourself. Just listen.

Then go to work on yourself. It takes time and persistence to smooth out your rough edges, but you can do it.

ACTION #2: Walk through your fear.

What are you afraid of? Confront the monster in your head painting all kinds of frightful failure scenarios, such as:

- I'm just too scared to step out of my comfort zone.
- What if I make a fool of myself?
- What if I fail?
- What if they don't like me?
- What if I'm not perfect?

Now reframe these negatives into positives by arguing with your internal monster.

- What's the worst that can happen? I'm not going to die.
- Am I going to let my fear hold me back from my dreams?

- Does being scared make me a bad speaker? No! Fear makes me try harder.
- Hmmmm, what is a "perfect speech" anyway?
- All I have to do is share my knowledge and valuable insights.
- If I make a mistake I'll just laugh and they'll like my vulnerability.

Then discard your personal self-absorption because communicating with others is not about you. It's about stepping into a positive presence with a spirit of service to others.

- This presentation is my gift to the folks in the audience.
- They need this powerful information I'm giving them.
- I can help them grow.
- It is my mission to help them grow.
- I'll explain my content as if we're just having a one-on-one conversation.
- Conversation! Of course! I talk to people all the time.
- I just need to lose myself in this fabulous content.
- This is how I help make the world a better place.
- I can do this!

Accept that the audience really wants you to succeed. They're with you, not against you. Just pretend they're actual people and have a conversation with them.

In fact, the more conversational and relaxed you feel, the less robotic and rehearsed you'll sound.

People want to listen to speakers who fill them with confidence, energy and enthusiasm because it gives them strength and hope.

Audiences don't identify with perfect people. In fact they dislike speakers who brag about how perfect they are.

And lastly remember that if you're uncomfortable it makes the audience feel uncomfortable too. So lighten up on yourself, kick back and enjoy sharing your value with them.

I want to pause here to emphasize that everything I've said applies to all "audiences" whether 1,000 strangers or one person.

These principles operate in all human interaction, everything from a job interview, to making a sale, to presenting a status report to your boss, or to talking with your spouse or child.

ACTION #3: Hang out with successful people and do what they do.

Seek out people who are making money doing the kind of work you want to get into. Ask their advice. Listen and apply it.

Be coachable!

Lately I've come to realize the value of coachability.

There are just gobs of reality shows on TV where people perform and are then given feedback by judges. One of my guilty pleasures is *Dancing with the Stars*.

I've noticed that the Olympic athlete contestants listen carefully and non-defensively to the judges' remarks, then return the following week showing substantial improvement.

Contrast this with some of the more temperamental "stars" who argue and defend themselves, then badmouth the judges back stage. They resist the advice so they don't improve.

Are you coachable?

It you are lucky enough to receive the gift of advice from some industry giant, please apply it. Trust me. No athlete makes it to the top of his sport unless s/he is coachable.

Above all, don't ask your loser friends and family for advice unless they are experts in your field. Strange as it seems, your well-meaning associates will actually work to discourage you from lifting yourself up.

Why? Because it means you're rejecting them and leaving behind the camaraderie you've shared together. It's human nature to take such actions personally and try to hold you back.

Successful people strive to be the best they can be. It's a never ending quest to constantly improve.

Unsuccessful people are content to just exist.

Expect better of yourself. It's definitely worth the effort.

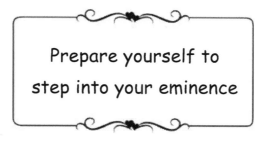

Prepare yourself to
step into your eminence

What Size Are Your Big Girl Panties?

*"The weak can never forgive.
Forgiveness is the attribute of the strong."*
Mahatma Gandhi

Let's face it, most people's big girl panties are bikinis.

Mine were.

For a long time, I never really forgave anyone for anything. I harbored grudges over various and sundry hurts. In fact for entertainment, I'd take one out, scratch the scab off and enjoy a refreshing bleed of self pity.

It takes intentional character to not only forgive the wrongs of others, real and imagined, but also to let go of blame and accusations. The way you know you've accomplished this feat is when you can laugh about the injury.

If you can't laugh, you haven't healed.

Back when our identical twin daughters went off to college, they chose totally different schools that matched their totally different personalities.

The Fashion Police daughter chose Texas Christian University where the co-eds are cosmetic-intensive, strikingly accessorized young women. Our other daughter, the Poster Child for the Homeless, opted for Texas A&M where fashion is apparently against the law.

When TCU visited her sister's campus sporting a cute outfit and full make-up, A&M exclaimed "Stop, you're embarrassing me!"

TCU started dating a nice young man. TCU Guy was playing golf with his childhood buddy, now turned Aggie, who asked "Do you know any girls at A&M rough enough to play ultimate Frisbee?"

TCU Guy responded, "No, but I'm dating a girl who has an A&M twin sister."

And thus it came to pass that these two unsuspecting and extremely fine young men, who grew up in the same small town with their mommies playing piano and organ at the same small church, and who were already distantly related by marriage, became brothers-in-law.

These days our family tree is looking more like a wreath.

Weddings

TCU tied the first knot, a modest June wedding with 465 of their closest friends.

A&M married the following June, with many of the same people invited to both ceremonies. Naturally, they wanted their weddings to be "totally different."

I assisted as a dutiful mother-of-the-bride (MOB) for two straight years.

During this time my Beloved and I learned that a wedding is simply a giant five hour party costing roughly the same as a year in college, or driving a Lexus off a cliff, but we're not bitter.

Following the honeymoon, the happy couple distanced themselves from both their families. This abrupt bombshell happened with NO warning. Everything was great, then suddenly they didn't call, they didn't write, we didn't see them although they lived just a few miles away.

Many otherwise normal and polite people, particularly mothers, assume that two families can both experience first-child-to-marry syndrome and nothing will change in their relationship with their offspring.

They begrudge their daughter or son every minute the new couple spends with The In-laws. Frequently this results in heinous holiday tug-o-wars that leave all parties bruised and bleeding.

Instead of accepting this detachment as part of the natural evolution of life, mothers can turn it into World War III. Mothers of daughters are also susceptible to believing their daughter is replacing them with her new mother-in-law.

Well anyway, this mother did.

After thoroughly humiliating myself with several emotional explosions that sent ripples through the whole family, I promised my daughter I would get over my junk.

But I didn't; I just pushed it down. I was a fraud, a hypocrite, a liar. I was practically a member of Congress.

A year passed and I threw myself into planning the second wedding.

One week before the A&M event, my cell phone rang as we wheeled into the mall parking lot to shop for a rehearsal dinner dress. It was my doctor. "It's malignant and we need you in here immediately!"

Now what would any rational MOB do? I have no idea. But I told my doctor I was busy.

This was my daughter's week to shine and I was not about to dim her spotlight with some petty little inconvenience like cancer.

Between tying bows on things and making extremely large final payments for wedding related expenditures, such as the dress, the caterer, the flowers, the chocolate fountain, the limos, the makeup artist, the hair stylist, the photographer, the videographer, and the movie director, there wasn't much time to spend sitting around being productively nervous.

The joyful wedding went off without a hitch. The bride was radiant, makeup covered most of the bridesmaids' tattoos, and the groom showed up.

This was a second (and third) union for both families, so acclimatization was uneventful. They can thank their siblings for being the first to marry off and take the brunt of it.

Cancer

The next week, as promised, I trudged into the hospital for assorted medical procedures and a lumpectomy. Due to the miracle of early detection, the breast cancer business is booming. In fact, if you don't know someone who's had breast cancer recently, you really need to get more friends.

Before the "it's malignant" call, I'd already endured three painfully squashy mammograms and a biopsy where I had to lie face down on a canvas sling and drop my boob through a hole in it – a position clearly designed by a tech with a porn problem.

Twenty-four hours before surgery I reported to the hospital nuclear medicine department where they injected blue dye into the offending boob. The dye migrates to the first or sentinel lymph node which gets removed during surgery.

The thing is it takes your body about a year to eliminate all of the dye. Gravity being involved, the dye drains down to the lowest point of your chest.

I always imagined that if I got a tattoo I'd like a butterfly on my butt instead of a blue nipple.

The next morning I report for surgery at 5:00 am. Surgery is always scheduled at ungodly hours so you can be even more miserable than you already are.

I was wheeled down to radiology for yet another mammogram. Only this time they poked a wire into the site to mark the exact location of the tumor. Then they curled up the remaining fifteen feet of cable and taped it to my chest.

Back in the OR, the surgeon handed me a Sharpie and told me to identify the affected boob. I scrawled, "Not here" on the right side and circled the left one with an arrow pointing to the protruding coat hanger dangling from my chest which was apparently invisible to the doctor's naked eye. And this is the very same person who was shortly going to open me up and dig around in there for buried treasure!

Surgery went well – another great nap. Biopsy results confirmed the cancer had not spread into the lymph system. The malignancy was declared Stage 1 which is considered greasy kids stuff in the disease world.

Radiation was next up on the menu, 36 treatments scheduled at 2:30 every afternoon.

At the appointed time, I presented myself wearing an open-down-the-front modestly garment which was immediately discarded. From that point on it's just me, my boob and four or five strangers arranging me, spread eagle on the radiation table. After a lot of button pushing and light flashing, they all ran from the room while the machine shot magic rays into my chest.

They always instructed me not to move during the endless expanse of time while I laid on the table, buck naked from the waist up. I amused myself by imagining what prostate radiation looks like.

That's the thing about childbirth and diseases of private body parts. You get accustomed to flopping your package out for anyone (doctors, nurses, technicians, roving janitors) to see it, discuss it, poke it and just generally publicly inspect it.

Because my appointment sliced the day in half, for the first time in my life, I powered down into the refreshing radiation lifestyle. I took to telling people I couldn't answer email or return phone calls because I had cancer.

Mornings consisted of exercising, then sitting outside reading, writing and pondering the meaning of life while also cooling down (which at my age takes about three hours what with hot flashes and all.)

Then I showered, primped, radiated and began thinking about dinner.

Letting Go

It was during this time of reflection that I seriously examined my harsh feelings from the previous year. I began to wonder why we as humans take so much pleasure in our emotional pain. If you didn't, wouldn't you eliminate it from your life?

We spend hours agonizing over the "Why me?" question, the theme song of self pity and the perfect gateway to victimhood. *Why is life so mean to me? I'm such a nice person! I don't deserve all the bad stuff that happens to me!*

Cleverly you ignore the corollary that you don't actually deserve all the good stuff either.

Eventually I got around to reframing the question into "Hmmmm, what does the Divine want me to learn from this experience?" And like a kick in the buttocks, the answer came back loud and clear, "I want you to forgive. You're acting like a selfish jerk. You really gotta grow up and learn how to forgive others and really, truly let it go!"

Whoa! Hold your horses and kiss my grits! That was harsh!

Let go of arrogant resentments? Stop wallowing in self-righteous justifications and destructive ruminations?

What will I do with all my free time?

I resisted the notion of letting go of my grudges because it felt like killing a dear friend who comprised a large segment of my interior life.

Then I made a startling connection – the venomous poison in my heart actually gave me cancer in my left breast. The spot appeared on mammograms for the previous five years, but it just happened to decide to grow the year I was consumed with fury and hurt.

Coincidence? Not hardly. There's a correlation.

Is this some sort of unscientific, woo woo explanation? Am I a complete and total moron?

Yes, of course I am, but not about the cancer causing properties of negativity and unforgiveness.

Here's some hard scientific research about this same theory. Prepare yourself – this will just sting a little.

Here it is: Negativity is bad for your health.

There now, that wasn't so painful, was it?

Here are some more scientifically proven facts:

- Negative people get older faster than positive people.

- Negative people make less money than positive people.

- Negative people are less successful than positive people.

- Negative people experience more heart disease, tumors and infections.

- Negative people are crabby.

There you have it, negativity causes TUMORS TO GROW!

Convinced, I set to work expunging the negativity from my heart and forgiving my daughter and son-in-law for the reprehensible act of crafting their own lives separate from mine.

I'd read that writing down your troubling thoughts and burning up the piece of paper makes the pain go "up in smoke."

So I extensively documented each and every woe I'd suffered, both real and exaggerated, meticulously documenting the time, place and dialogue of who said what, including quotation marks and large numbers of exclamation points.

I labored to re-imagine each and every moment of this now legendary saga. Then I proofed it for spelling and punctuation.

It took days to compose this magnum opus – because as the saying goes, it was a real "piece of work."

Then in the back yard I worshipfully constructed an altar from a rusty wrought iron bench supporting a chipped clay pot.

On an appointed day at an appointed time, I knelt, I prayed, and I ceremonially set fire to the Manuscript of Woe.

The sacred flames rose up to the sky, nearly igniting an overhanging branch. And when the smoke cleared, I felt – NOTHING! I was still just as upset as before!

Darn! Where is the cleansing balm of release? The liberating freedom from retribution? The storied wonders of forgiveness?

Sadly I realized letting go was going to be harder than I thought, mainly because I was a proud professional martyr.

Humbled, I set to work rewriting the script. This time it was a little less self-indulgent, a little more factual and a bit shorter. The flames ascended, the smoke circled, and… the unforgiveness lessened by a millimeter, which for those of you unfamiliar with the metric system is technically defined as "not much."

I repeated this tedious cycle seven or eight more times, narrowly averting a massive forest fire. Apparently my heart wasn't just stone; it was pure granite. At length and at last though, I tired of the struggle and finally my unforgiveness skulked away into the underbrush.

My big girl panties graduated to briefs.

Hurts come in all different shapes and sizes. Human beings intentionally inflict horrible and unforgivable physical and emotional damage upon each other. Many people have suffered far more than me. But pain is pain, regardless of cause. Unfortunately, I was a master at escalating small resentments into a Greek tragedy of drama and suffering.

What can be learned from this experience? Many things. I learned cancer can be a gift. I know I am not the only one who has thanked their cancer for initiating a major life course correction.

What is it about human nature that we can be so dense and self-absorbed it takes a frightening physical ailment to get our attention refocused on a much needed habit improvement?

Most gratifying was watching my child, my first to get married, become such a wonderful adult who not only put her husband first, just as she should, but also patiently allowed her mother to process her junk. I guess I raised those kids alright after all.

I'm also grateful for the enriching relationship forged with my son-in-law's family. What a tragedy it would have been if my issues got in the way of enjoying shared time with our mutual grandchildren!

I heartily recommend forgiveness and truly letting go of your pain. It changed my life – and thus the lives of my entire family.

Maturity Killing Assumptions

ASSUMPTION #1: Holding on to emotional pains can't physically hurt me.

Wake up, McFly! Feel free to conduct your own research of the current science on this topic if you need more convincing.

Dr. Martin Seligman, known as the father of positive psychology, has studied optimism and pessimism for over 40 years and probably knows more about it than anyone. He's published lots of user-friendly books on the subject. My favorite and the one that transformed my thinking is *Learned Optimism*.

ASSUMPTION #2: I will forgive. But I won't forget.

Don't kid yourself. Not forgetting is definitely NOT forgiving. It's easy to say, "I forgive you" and much more character building to really, really, really let it go.

The truth is you must let go of something to grow and there is no growth without change. Up level your game here and do some growing by letting go. You also need to forgive yourself.

ASSUMPTION #3: I'm entitled to hurt the person who hurt me.

Retribution requires no moral fiber whatsoever. Suck it up and take the high road. It's much less crowded and infinitely more pleasurable. Plus, it's kinder to your family, friends and especially your body.

ASSUMPTION #4: I am entitled to feel upset when things don't happen the way they "ought to."

Yes, AND... free speech entitles you to falsely yell "fire!" in a crowded theatre, but that's not smart.

We're learning how to combat the slings and arrows of outrageous fortune with humor. The sooner you laugh, the faster you heal.

Shorten the time between the hurt and the laughter. It makes the journey so much more enjoyable.

ASSUMPTION #5: Marriages are happy occasions and should effortlessly knit families together.

Setting aside all the "Bridezilla" stories and shrill arguments over insanely trivial details like whether there should be strawberry or raspberry cake filling, weddings are happy occasions.

They celebrate the lifelong union of two people both of whom are members of larger clans who have drawn a line in the sand and declared their allegiance to either the bride or groom in the form of seat selection. Frequently the MOB and MOG shoot poison darts at each other across the aisle and must be restrained by the father of the bride or "Daddy Wedding Bucks" who in the process rips his rented tuxedo and quickly calculates that's another $497 down the drain.

All families are composed of human beings and people will always find some territory to growl over. The bickering won't hurt you if you're looking down on it from your perch on the high road.

ASSUMPTION #6: Nursing my pain is a fun and pleasurable activity.

As humans deeply involved in ourselves, we don't expend energy doing things we don't want to do. We make up elaborate excuses in order to avoid doing anything we're either too disinterested in doing or too lazy to care about.

We're also really averse to pain. Remember how you break out in a sweat just before you get a shot? So if you're spending a lot of time, emotion, and therapeutic shopping dollars on wallowing in a hurt then, trust me here, at some level you're deriving pleasure and satisfaction from it.

Confront and admit this pleasure so you can grow up.

Maturity Enriching Actions

ACTION #1: Separate fact from fiction.

Most of our negative thoughts are just that—thoughts, not facts. Write down all the negative junk the idiot in your head is saying. Most likely the only exercise your idiot gets is jumping to conclusions.

Then evaluate these statements to see if they're factual. You can bet the statements aren't true any time you see words like *never, always, worst, ever,* etc. Are you *never* going to find a solution to your problem? Does it *always* happen? If it's really such an intractable problem, then why are you wasting your time beating your head against the wall?

ACTION #2: Replace negative thoughts with positive ones.

Identifying and labeling your thoughts as *thoughts* by separating them from true facts is one way to help you leap off the train of negativity and land on the trampoline of joy.

Another way is to tell the idiot in your head to "shut up." Arguing with the idiot works wonders in getting from negative to positive thinking AND is a scientifically proven method recommended by four out of five psychologists who find your rubbish so boring they are willing to pay you to please go away.

ACTION #3: Write down five gratitudes every day.

So one day some therapists were sitting around laughing about how screwed up their patients were because they (the patients) actually followed the advice of their (the therapists') and journaled every day. Then one of them said, "Hey Phil, do you suppose it actually matters what they write about or could they just as easily be making a grocery list?" and Phil responded in his most reflective voice, "Gee Fred, I don't know. What do you think?"

These questions flew back and forth for several hours because therapists have all the questions, but none of the answers. Finally a guy at the next table said, "For god's sake shut up and go test it!"

They went out and found some newly depressed people, divided them into three groups and told them they absolutely, positively had to journal every day. Group 1 wrote about events. Group 2 was assigned feelings. And Group 3, being the slow learning group, just had to write down things they were grateful for.

At the end of the test, Groups 1 and 2 were still just as depressed and the therapists were thrilled because that meant journaling had no therapeutic value and thus they could continue prescribing it.

But the dummies in Group 3 screwed up the test results and showed remarkable improvement in reducing their depression. The moral to this story is: writing down gratitudes really works to lighten your load.

I personally recommend writing down five new gratitudes every day because three is too few and ten is too many. Frankly, I just can't be that grateful.

Also, notice the word "new." You can't continually be grateful for the same stuff every day like your lovely family and brilliant children and beautiful home. NO!

You have to go out and find new stuff to be grateful for – like the person who let you cut in line because you were in a hurry and only had five items or the yellow Toyota that nearly, but didn't actually hit you or the welcoming smile of your barista at Starbucks.

ACTION #4: Learn a wise lesson from every experience.

Many permanently depressed and unforgiving people learn all the wrong lessons in life.

One useful strategy is to sort bad events into piles labeled "this is just a temporary, not my fault event" and "this is permanent, definitely my fault event." The negative idiot in your head generally lumps everything bad into the "permanent, my fault" heap.

For example, if your boss unexpectedly snarls at you about something that is clearly not your fault, then a wise lesson to learn is "My boss is having a bad day."

However, if your boss reprimands you for being late to work five of the last ten days, and your idiot dismisses the correction as "my boss is just having a bad day" then your idiot is an idiot. Being late 50% of the time is definitely your fault, so fix it.

Learn to distinguish between self-defeating blaming thoughts and positive fixing the situation thoughts.

The key to happiness is letting go of hurt. Seriously bad things can happen to nice people. Letting go of the anger, hurt and grief will keep you from growing old, bitter and diseased.

I heartily recommend forgiveness. Just imagine how delightful your life would be if you laughed at negative thoughts and grew into size XXL big girl panties.

Give it a whirl. The resulting joy might surprise you.

Complete forgiveness
requires letting go
completely

Smile While You Still Have Teeth

"The best way of removing negativity
is to laugh and be joyous"
David Icke

Whining wasn't my native tongue. I only became bi-lingual during my rebellious youth. It was the late sixties and while other more progressive thinkers were protesting injustice, hallucinating at Woodstock, and conscientiously burning bras, I was fully engaged in discovering the fulfillment of chronic complaining.

My family of origin maintained strict virginity about whining. Every evening at the dinner table, in between the vocabulary games, spelling tests, and history lessons, my father forced us to recount at least one good thing that happened that day.

Daddy allowed no mention of bad things. On camping trips, he insisted that it was the hardships that made it fun. The freezing nights, the pouring rain, flash floods, congealed food on metal plates, bears in the garbage and of course blankets of mosquitoes – I'm tearing up just remembering all those good times.

Only upon entering the workforce did I discover the joys of incessant grumbling, the official language of adulthood. Or was it victimhood?

I was eighteen and eager to make my mark in the world by rejecting as bogus everything my parents taught me. To earn my way through college, I took a job as a long distance telephone operator at The Mighty Phone Company, primarily because I got to sit down on the job.

There we sat, 100 women elbow to elbow on a long switchboard the length of a football field. The large, heavy headset put a dent in my Aqua-Net intensive bubble hairdo. For those of you whose baby pictures are in color, Aqua-Net was a shellac-based hair spray that came in a half-gallon size aerosol can costing 98¢ at the Safeway and was capable of invincibly gluing your Jackie Kennedy coif to your head.

I think Aqua-Net was solely responsible for global warming prior to the invention of environmentalists.

There's something about estrogen in confined spaces that causes it to explode into a mushroom cloud of kvetching. It was my first exposure to pervasive, unrestrained griping, and these women were professionals.

As with all new languages, at first I just listened to the grammar and inflection, the tone and texture, the rhythm and melody of the dialect around me. Then I hesitantly ventured a simple sentence, "It's too cold in here."

Within a few short months I could add a passive aggressive twist, "They should know it's too cold."

Later and with practice I could assert a tentative accusation, "They keep it too cold in here on purpose."

But it took a long time to master the full fledged character assassin, and helplessness, so favored by expert linguists, "They're too stupid to know it's cold and too mean to care."

The problem was I never truly fit in with the whining women of the headset world because my heart wasn't into the game. I was just a foreigner with an accent because somewhere along the way I'd ring the kindly supervisor and ask her to please adjust the thermostat.

I also began to fear that if I didn't get out of this Twilight Zone of negativity I would spontaneously morph into a crabby old woman, gain 50 pounds and wear pink stretch pants.

The opportunity to escape presented itself in the form of a promotion. As I neared college graduation, the evil boss, now turned supportive and nurturing advisor, offered me entry into a management training program specially designed for brilliant young female college graduates such as myself.

It promised that if you were really dedicated, worked hard and ate your Wheaties, after ten or fifteen years you might – just maybe – be promoted to second-line management.

Male graduates entered a totally separate program with the expectation that if you did okay, showed up for work fairly regularly and weren't caught in flagrante doing it with a female employee, you were guaranteed a third-line management position in three years.

I was overjoyed by this new and thrilling career as a "junior executive." However, all too soon I began to notice inequities. Utilizing my newly acquired language skills, I whined incessantly about these issues to my colleagues, my family, my friends, and strangers on the bus unable to flee my shrill refrain.

At length and at last, as my frustrations reached a fever pitch, an interview with the most senior executive in a five state region was arranged.

I drove downtown, took the elevator to the gazillionth floor and meekly entered the deeply carpeted, hallowed office of His Highness, The Most Holy Phone Company Potentate.

Somewhat like an archangel, this very nice white-haired gentleman patiently explained to me that:

a) The reason women couldn't be promoted higher than second-level management was because they cry, so…

b) That's why there was a separate program for men with different advancement expectations, plus…

c) He really appreciated my work down in the trenches of ignorance, but…

d) I would never be happy at The Mighty Phone Company because it couldn't change fast enough to please me.

That last nugget was actually a quite valuable insight.

I told him I appreciated his time and penetrating wisdom; then proceeded down to the first floor to resign.

By the way, ten years later I received a check for $72.13 as my compensation from a multi-million dollar class action lawsuit settlement over this very same junior executive program.

Taking my whining skills to the next job, I unknowingly leapt out of the slow-boiling Phone Company pot into the flaming fires of a seriously antiquated insurance company.

It was now 1972, but this company sported a corporate culture reminiscent of a 1940's movie only without the form-fitting tweed suits and snappy dialogue.

A signature policy of this esteemed institution was the rule that every woman must occupy a secretarial chair with no arms, specifically to cozy up to the equally mandatory typewriter. Each woman was expected to be constantly vigilant with fingers at the ready in case a roaming male (including the stock boy) needed to dictate an emergency memo.

All men directed the universe from magnificent chairs with arms, their innate superiority never sullied by proximity to a typewriter. I accepted the inevitability of the situation and enthusiastically engaged in endless griping with the other women in residence.

Then my boss proposed I represent the company in the city-wide contest to be the next lovely and radiant Miss Philanthropy. The vulgar anomaly of complaining about gender-based unfair treatment, but happily embracing a gauche female figurehead position escaped my notice.

I completed an application which included among other things, my body measurements. On judging day I entered a room of ancient geezers, which I later realized were just stalwart men in their mid-forties.

They asked a few questions, then requested I promenade so they could inspect my philanthropic qualifications. Surprisingly and in spite of my AA cups, I won.

At the press conference where they announced the winner, I stepped to the open microphone. Suddenly seized with a dawning awareness of women's liberation, and heady from my victory, I mentioned that boobs shouldn't be a qualification for such a venerated position.

This casual remark made national news and generated a flurry of press calls which I graciously received, pontificating at length from the throne of my secretarial chair.

The men were not amused. My career at that insurance company was doomed.

Next I stumbled into another insurance company where, Praise the Lord, I met my mentor, a slightly older golden boy sent as oversight from the prosperous holding company.

Unfazed by the fact that I was female, he taught me how to research a problem, craft a solution, successfully present it to C-level executives and then marshal system-wide resources to implement it.

My career was now exciting and challenging. Since my beloved engineer worked 55 hour weeks and we hadn't reproduced yet, my Aqua-net coif and I bonded to this work like bubble gum on a shoe.

For almost fifteen years I tagged along on the coat tails of my more successful and talented mentor, but always as an independent contractor so he wouldn't have to face the daunting challenge of trying to insert me into the all-male executive social structure of banking and insurance.

Finally at the ripe old age of 36, I was initiated into the boys club, becoming Chief Operating Officer of a $1.5 billion mortgage bank.

I was HOT stuff (and most likely insufferably arrogant.) I flew around the country on the bank's private jet, headed a workforce of 350 and measured my worth by the number of zeroes on my pay checks.

As it turns out, I was elevated to this exalted position because this subsidiary of the holding company was teetering on the edge of bankruptcy and the owner needed a scapegoat. Enter me, a female puffed up with pride in solving complex problems in large organizations. Pay her a lot of money and set her up for almost certain failure.

I unwittingly and eagerly accepted the challenge and waltzed into the cesspool.

After six months of fifteen hour days, we hauled this train wreck of a company out of the ditch of bankruptcy and back up on the rails of functional incompetency. Even with the long hours and now three small children, it was one of the most fulfilling work experiences of my life.

My Beloved and I decided to celebrate with a 4,000 mile driving vacation to Disneyland. Our enthusiasm for the insane prospect of being trapped in the car with three barely potty-trained preschoolers stands as stark testament to the desperation of our lives.

For the last 3½ years the only time we had gotten out of the house was when my Beloved and I, accompanied by all three munchkins, celebrated date night at the Piggly Wiggly.

This vacation will live in the annals of Barab history, rivaling the legendary Chevy Chase's movie *Vacation* for sheer number of catastrophes.

We'd just taken delivery on our very first Suburban – the national car of Texas. One hundred miles into the trip we diagnosed the annoying vibration of the truck as misaligned front tires. However, my Beloved refused to stop and pay to get it fixed because back home at the dealership repairs were free.

Onward we shimmied, destination after destination creating vacation memories from the fun of hardships. Amarillo sported a hail storm of biblical proportions. Carlsbad Caverns flooded. Mesa Verde burned.

And then there's the excess body substance issues routinely associated with toddlers. Across the New Mexico desert, torrential rains confined us in the car with windows closed during a particularly virulent outbreak of smelly diarrhea.

In Arizona, a heinous travel potty accident deposited its contents all over the back seat of our brand new vehicle.

At the San Diego Zoo, a peacock pooped on my Beloved's head.

The piece de resistance occurred when our son began vomiting pancakes in the Disneyland parking lot and we spent the entire day in the emergency room.

In Anaheim, while the kids napped I snuck off to check in at the office. Due to the absence of cell phones in this still prehistoric time, I sought the services of a pay phone located on an exceedingly hot and noisy street corner.

"Hello?" I shouted into the receiver. "This is Anne."

"Oh yes, Mr. Owner wants to speak with you. I'll connect you."

Mr. Owner came on the line. "Say Anne, thanks for all your hard work over at the mortgage bank."

"Oh thank you. It was all my team."

"Yeah that's what I thought, too. Plus we can't continue having a woman in such a high position of responsibility so we're letting you go."

Just like that. Fired!

I dissolved into a squashy heap of self-pity, anguish and – you guessed it – whining, my highly articulate, one-size-fits-all language of adversity.

How dare the world be unfair to ME! I'm a nice person! I'm a hard worker! I'm smarter than everybody else!

And yet, there I stood, sweaty, sticky, and out of a job.

Actually I was deeply shamed and humiliated. This was the beginning of the ignoble thrift failure. Eighteen months later if you hadn't been fired from a savings & loan, then you just didn't rank as a high powered decision maker worthy of blame.

But since I was ahead of the curve, I tucked in my tail, crept into my cave and hid. It was the most devastating experience of my young life.

And yes, at last something genuinely unfair and worth complaining about had happened to me.

In fact the company lawyers told me I had grounds to sue but the owner might not have the money to pay a settlement and I would probably never work in the industry again.

Not long after that conversation, the owner was sent to jail for his part in the thrift industry collapse. Although this might be an example of "what goes around comes around," I didn't relish his fall from power because he was actually pretty nice guy.

Many years later, in a remarkable twist of fate, while I served on the school board, I handed his son his high school graduation diploma.

Life is funny – and sometimes unfair.

Slowly it began to dawn on me that complaining had no effect on a situation's outcome. It didn't change anything – except me. Chronic complaining intensified my anger, pain, self pity and crafted a robust pride in victimhood. But it didn't get my job back.

Then a miracle occurred. I discovered the optimism/pessimism work of Dr. Martin Seligman. I read his book *Learned Optimism* which contained an innocent little test.

Most people love these things and I'm no exception. However, the way you scored it was complicated and took a third of the book to explain. The scores resulted in a continuum ranging from a negative eight if you were really pessimistic up to a positive eight if you're exceptionally optimistic. I scored – wait for it – negative seven.

WHAT??? I was stunned because I've always thought I was wildly optimistic. But it turns out I'm just perky.

The rest of the book described how to teach your brain to think positive thoughts. Dr. Seligman's theory postulates that optimism can be learned by arguing with the idiot in your head who constantly spews a steady stream of venom into your psyche. There's also a lot of data about how negativity produces higher quantities of:

- Stress

- Unhappiness

- Depression

- Illness

- Helplessness AND

- Halitosis

I just made that last one up.

OMG, recreational whining so I could fit in and be popular produced noxious side effects! Who knew? Chastised and kind of desperate, I resolved to apply Dr. Seligman's principles. It was life changing.

Time passed; three years to be exact. I happened upon the book again and thought I'd take another whirl at the test. Remember that complex scoring system? I'd forgotten the rules so I couldn't fudge. My final score this time was – drum roll, please – positive three! Woo Hoo!

As I rejoiced over this victory I began to assess my current life condition.

- My relationship with my Beloved was better than ever before.

- My relationship with my three-count 'em-three junior high school teenagers was flourishing.

- My business relationships were productive and satisfying.

- Best of all, nothing on my body hurt!

Scientists now know that stress can take up residence in:

- Your musculoskeletal system (tension headaches, hunched shoulders, back pain, TMJ, tendonitis muscle, plus autoimmune diseases like arthritis and lupus)

- Your nervous system (heart pounding, high blood pressure, clogged arteries, anxiety, depression, low libido and poor sleep) AND

- Your digestive system.

Since The Phone Company and my acquaintance with victim language, I'd suffered blinding headaches and crippling stomach cramps. Doctors continually diagnosed the pains as acute hypochondria. This was before the invention of acid reflux and irritable bowel syndrome.

Now as I reflected, I realized that arguing with the idiot in my head had really reduced stress and pretty much eliminated all those side effects. Also, by scrapping the complaining lifestyle, I'd freed up a lot of conversational energy I could put to use in positive problem solving. How very marvelous!

Talking about the good things that happen to you and refusing to give air time to the bad is actually endorsed by the American Psychiatric Association.

It had taken only just the twenty-five painful years for me to realize Daddy was right!

One time, in the midst of a full-scale depression my therapist told me I should journal daily. I hated that. Writing with regularity was a practice that so far had eluded me, although goodness knows I'd tried.

As a young girl I received a pink plastic diary with a little lock on it to protect from the prying eyes of my siblings all the torment, angst and deeply emotional secrets I would surely experience and write about. I made an entry on the first page like "Today is January 1st and we ate black eyed peas."

Then there'd be a gap of say five years before I wrote another nugget of wisdom like "I'm in ninth grade now and I love Frank Watts" who ended up making license plates in Huntsville, but back then I thought he was dreamy.

Frank sported a heavily Brylcreemed duck tail hairdo later immortalized by The Fonz and nifty horned rimmed glasses that made his eyes look like tiny black dots. Come to think of it, I've always found four-eyed guys sexy because I also married one. But back to journaling…

About this time I discovered a scientific study that writing down things you're grateful for really dispels negativity. Since I was fishing around for motivational topics to speak on, I decided to test out the effectiveness of this gratitude thing.

I began arising at 30 minutes early every morning so I could meditate and journal. There I sat at 0-dark-hundred trying to be grateful for stuff.

I started out giving thanks for flowers and blue sky and birdies. Then we went on a mission trip to Guatemala and I returned intensely grateful for soap and hot water. I stuck with that for about two months and then thought, "Hmmm maybe that's a bit shallow."

I was busy congratulating myself on the whole experiment when alas I discovered you couldn't just be grateful for the same old things every day. So instead of writing "I'm grateful for my charming home, exceptionally lovely offspring and most especially for my Beloved's paycheck" you had to think up new stuff all the time. Uh Oh…

What's "magic" about writing <u>different</u> gratitudes every day is that it trains your mind to look for the good all around you. It takes absolutely NO talent to see the bad; we are hard-wired to sense threats.

It requires skill and conscious effort to look for the good in every situation and most especially in others, even smelly old Aunt Edna.

The simple practice of writing down daily gratitudes got me through my years as a professional mother-of-the-bride, breast cancer, the deaths of my mother, my mother-in-law and my favorite aunt, settling a family dispute over Mom's estate, a divorce in the family (not ours) and the heartbreak of psoriasis – just the garden variety stuff of life.

I highly recommend it.

Negativity leads to pessimism which promotes more stress which produces more depression which causes lots of health issues which make you feel hopeless and that you life is out of control.

Positive thinking produces optimism which reduces stress which cultivates more joy which encourages better health which fosters a sense of life mastery.

Your choice, but positivity sounds a whole lot more appealing to me.

Complainer Assumptions

ASSUMPTION #1: Life should be fair!

Fair is just another nasty four letter word. I spent a heck of a lot of time grieving over unfairness. But ultimately you've got to grow up.

Even in America, the home of the brave and the whiny, unfair stuff still happens. This pitfall is based upon the unfounded notion that yeah, yeah, life may be unfair for others, but I'm special and I'm entitled to better!

Griping about how "That's not fair!" is as futile as chasing after the wind. A much more productive approach is to laugh, heal, learn from the unfairness and become stronger.

In retrospect, I'm really grateful for the experience of being fired. I wasn't handling power humbly or gracefully. Apparently the Lord realized I was such a bonehead He needed to whack me with a really large stick to get my attention.

Life isn't fair. Deal with it. Learn from it. Grow beyond it.

ASSUMPTION #2: Venting helps me process issues and get over them.

Perhaps. However, tediously rehashing how your daddy didn't hug you enough or the boss doesn't appreciate your efforts enough or the barista didn't top your skinny white chocolate mocha with whip enough is not therapeutic processing. I don't care how you dress up this dog; it's still just a pity party.

ASSUMPTION #3: My negative observations help others avoid pitfalls.

Trust me on this one, your tacky comments are definitely NOT making the world a better place. You're just another mindless whiner.

Scanning the landscape for threats is embedded in our DNA. But let's be clear, you're not sighting saber-tooth tigers here. You're engaged in the petty practice of observing the pimples of life.

Take a listen to yourself every now and then. You'll see you're never complaining about yourself because of course you are perfect. Instead you're always finding imperfections in others based upon hasty fault-finding that they:

- Didn't act the way you thought they should OR

- Didn't show you enough respect OR

- Didn't read your mind.

Please, your whining is not helping anyone; you're just stuck on Assumption #1 that life should be fair!

ASSUMPTION #4: But MY life is harder than yours.

Hey, adversity isn't a contest but chronic complainers treat it like it is.

I met a woman at a speaking engagement whose radiant face drew me to her. She thanked me for my presentation and casually remarked that today was the ten year anniversary of her daughter's murder. She was not whining. She was radiantly happy and laughing. How does your teeny weenie gripe stack up in that competition?

I met another gal named Elsa who was born in Germany in 1932. Elsa and her family spent WWII dodging bombs while searching for the safest shelter so they could be liberated by the Americans instead of the Russians. (Good choice, Elsa.) She, who indeed had a hard life, made the comment, "Kids today don't have it easy like we did."

Everybody's got something. Stop playing the "My life is harder than yours" game.

ASSUMPTION #5: I'm just being realistic.

Listen up, all you Grumps and Grumpettes. Grousing endlessly about how things "ought to be" does NOT make you a better person. It turns you into a bitter, cantankerous old grouch.

Sadly, whiners serious about their art are generally humorless as well. Frankly, I've never met a chronic complainer who was happy.

Complainer Transformative Actions

ACTION #1: Accept inconsequential things without judgment.

You do not need to have an opinion about everything in the universe. Not having an opinion protects you from a lot of misery.

126

When our son, the child formerly called Jeff, changed his name to Mandala, it was an excellent example of something to get upset about. However, accepting it without judgment helped me breeze through the transition. Now I make him call me Momdala.

ACTION #2: Eliminate the word "should" from your vocabulary.

Spoiler alert: use of the word "should" indicates you're getting ready to either:

- Give unsolicited advice as in "Girl, you should tell him to make his own coffee!" OR

- Render a most likely erroneous judgment about something that doesn't matter, as in "They should know I don't like my coffee this hot!"

Who are "they"? Were "they" supposed to read your mind? If so, isn't reading your mind an invasion of privacy?

The only acceptable use of "should" is when it's preceded by the pronoun "I" as in "I should shut and stop complaining about the damn coffee."

ACTION #3: Write down five gratitudes every day.

Recent scientific findings declare that gratitude:

- Maximizes life satisfaction

- Bolsters self-worth

- Helps cope with stress and trauma

- Strengthens relationships

- Decreases envy, anger, bitterness, greed

- Teaches you to quit taking things for granted

- Improves your desire to help others AND

- Helps you adjust, move on and begin anew.

Sign me up!

I have sampled the complaining lifestyle and suffered many of its unfortunate side effects. I suggest you release your inner snark and laugh your way into becoming a joyful contribution to the human race.

You will feel better. And amazingly, life will go better too. Happiness will cause you to exclaim – in the immortal words of Sally Fields, "You like me! You really like me!"

Unfair stuff happens
Laugh about it

Are We There Yet?

*"The cool thing about being famous is
traveling. I have always wanted to travel
across seas, like to Canada and stuff."*
Britney Spears

The trouble with travel is that you have to leave home to do it.

We live in a wonderful world full of beauty, charm, adventure and some really smelly people with crazy customs.

Take Spain for instance. All the businesses close from 2 to 5 pm so everybody can TAKE a NAP followed by dinner at 10 pm. Then the evening paseo begins and at <u>midnight</u> the streets are clogged with kids running around and families pushing strollers.

In America if parents were out strolling with infants at midnight they'd be arrested for child abuse – or mugged.

So first of all when do these people find time for school or work? And second, why doesn't American business allow three hour naps?

My Beloved husband and I are intrepid travelers. We've been to all 50 states in the US and 32 or 33 countries, depending upon whether you count Texas as both a state and a country.

America is a great place to visit, mainly because it is conveniently located in the USA. It's chock full of many interesting sights like the Empire State Building, the Grand Canyon and Whataburger (motto: a square meal on a round bun.)

Back in the 50's my three brothers and I were jammed into the back seat of our trusty wood-paneled station wagon for a driving vacation of mythic proportions when we happened upon one of the very first Whataburger establishments in some god-forsaken desert town in west Texas. My younger brother marveled at the cleverness of that motto endlessly for 5,000 miles. We couldn't shut him up. But I digress...

Because my Beloved's place of employment required mass vacation the first two weeks in July, every year we'd pile our three kids into the mighty Suburban (the national car of Texas) for several thousand miles of fun-filled family togetherness.

We particularly favored Nature in the form of national parks of which the US has an abundance, 58 to be exact. Not many other countries are so heavily into the National Park concept.

Canada boasts several including Banff, Jasper, and the ever popular Head-Smashed-In Buffalo Jump National Park.

While the kids were young we forced them to "appreciate nature" up close and personal. We figured Nature with her wild animals, snakes, freezing lakes, creepy crawly things, outdoor Porta Potties, poisonous berries, and steep rocky ledges was infinitely safer for small kids than big city civilization.

As teenagers they complained mightily about the injustice of long hikes, rafting raging rivers, climbing real mountains (versus the weenie rock walls in sporting goods stores) and riding horses, cable cars, four-wheelers, house boats and jet skis. But we persevered.

We sighted bears, beavers, swans, buffalo, moose, elk, deer, coyotes, sea lions, marmots, wolves, and caribou and learned to identify their various droppings after we stepped in them.

Speaking of droppings, my Beloved amassed a huge photo album of me emerging from rest stops across the nation, from sea to shining sea.

In the beginning of a vacation, before our kidneys toughened up, my Beloved graciously allowed pit stops every few hundred miles. But by the end of the trip after we'd developed steel-reinforced bladders, we were capable of driving for days with nary a tinkle.

And that's the thing about men, when Dad gets in The Zone and is "making time" he doesn't stop for meals, poop, historical markers or appendicitis. Fast food is the only sustenance he allows mainly because in the drive-thru he only has to slow to twenty.

Museums

Everywhere we went my Beloved insisted we visit museums and read all the little plaques and study all the dioramas. Then back in the car he'd quiz everybody about the museum's Major Concept. As a result of this quest to learn about all things Nature, Art and Science, we've seen some real doozies of museum-like establishments.

For example, crossing the New Mexico and Arizona desert we passed 200 miles of billboards advertizing a MUST SEE GIANT FIRE-BREATHING PREHISTORIC NOT TO BE MISSED MONSTER, only 167 miles to go, only 163 miles to go, only 159 miles to go – which, when we finally got there, turned out to be a rather largish gecko.

Other really goofy small time museums we've inspected include:

- The Hatfields and McCoys museum with pictures of an ever dwindling supply of male family members sporting an ever dwindling supply of teeth.

- The Twenty Mule Team Borax Museum with a life-size replica of – you guessed it – twenty mules hitched together. Also, we discovered Borax is an actual scientific element, and not just laundry soap.

- The Dinosaur Tracks Museum consisting of several Barca-lounger sized molds of dinosaur tracks.

- The UFO Museum with memorabilia from the flying saucer crash in Roswell, NM, containing among other things, an authentic replica of a genuine alien space ship made out of what appeared to be aluminum foil.

- The Hell Museum composed of dried lumpy black lava that would be really painful to walk on with bare feet. Taking the Fundamentalist high road, the kids refused to get out of the car at that one.

- A zoo in Singapore featuring such exotic specimens as a beaver, a yellow eyed jackal and a Labrador retriever. It was during a show at this very same zoo that the MC selected my Beloved from among the thousands in attendance primarily because he was:

- Wearing a red shirt
- The only white guy in a sea of brown faces
- Dozing

Under the duress of the moment he stepped down to the stage whereupon the quite commanding female MC (with the help of several burly attendants) draped a fifteen foot giant python around my Beloved's neck. Later he remarked that he was less afraid of the snake than the lady MC.

Perhaps the tedium of museums is an acquired taste. We're discovering that our sons-in-law don't share our fascination with all things museum.

For example, at say the Metropolitan Museum in New York boasting over 3,000,000 units of art it takes the SILs upwards of 63 whole minutes to see everything. Then they while away the remaining hours waiting for us in the snack bar discussing important ball scores.

Europe is absolutely jam packed with giant cathedrals housing mass quantities of Art. Back in the Middle Ages when they were building all these massive structures, pictures depicting biblical scenes were the only art subjects allowed by The Church. So today you're really up a creek without a paddle if you're unfamiliar with the plot in *The Bible*.

Then the Renaissance hit and Michelangelo and his buddies blew into town, starting a fashion trend featuring large muscular naked people. For the next 500 years artists fell over each other painting fabulous scenes of war, love, nudity and fruit.

In fact, many of the war scenes depict people who forgot their clothes charging into battle and carrying fruit, thereby cleverly combining all the disciplines in one bizarre and illogical painting.

It seems to me that if you had time to remember your sandals, and spear you'd also want to throw on a pair of shorts.

Generals even rode magnificent horses into battle buck naked (the generals, not the horses.) Talk about saddle sores. I'm a girl and even I don't want to imagine the chafing.

Then modern art got invented and not only can you not figure out if they're wearing clothes, you can't tell if it's a person or a washing machine.

Souvenirs

For some tourists shopping is the main purpose of travel. Souvenir shops are all jam packed with the same types of useless objects. I mean, what's up with all those little silver spoons you find all over the east coast? Or genuine hand-crafted native objects with the words "Made in Bangladesh" stamped on the bottom?

We purchase this "must have" stuff to show our unfortunate friends and family and to prove that we absolutely, positively were THERE. Sadly, the trip home in your suitcase causes most of these priceless keepsakes to morph into even more hideous and tacky trinkets.

This is particularly true of garments purchased from faraway places. That sensational Hawaiian flowered shirt looks idiotic when you prance around wearing it at the neighborhood barbeque.

Or what about the charming gingham apron you purchased in the back hills of Tennessee that, when you put it on back home, makes you look like Minnie Pearl.

In our family we've collected T-shirts mainly because they're cheap and easy to pack. However once home these are sometimes so tasteless we hesitate to wear them even doing yard work. For example:

- Snorkel Naked
- Kiss my Butte
- There's a name for people without beards – Women
- Visit beautiful Guantanamo Bay

You might be wondering how two adults and three kids could stand to be in such close proximity to each other for extended periods of time? Here are some tips:

- The truck was fifteen feet long so parents maintained a minimum distance of ten feet from their children at all times.

- There was a strict "No Whining" rule for kids and its corollary the "No Nagging" rule for parents.

- Fines were imposed for "Failure to Wake Up, Sit Up and Appreciate Scenery" because we'd driven all those miles to get there, damn it.

Then eventually our children grew up, went to college and thankfully drifted away to their own lives, leaving my Beloved and me to our own devices.

Europe

Since we'd seen so much of America we began to cast our travel eyes on distant shores.

In our first tentative step into Europe we toured Switzerland, Germany and Austria known as the "safe and neat countries."

I'm a huge fan of movie musicals and managed to pass this passion to the next generation. In fact our daughters tested potential marriage candidates for their movie musical IQ by asking complex questions like: "What is the name of the famous musical that contains the song *Ooooo-klahoma*?" After polling his entire office, the mechanical engineer responded *South Pacific* and was promptly disqualified as mate material.

So naturally, I just had to take *The Sound of Music* tour in Salzburg. Yes indeed, we visited all the "historic" sights of that ageless film including:

- The road Julie Andrews sang and danced down on the way to the huge von Trapp family mansion which is now a private institute that is sick and tired of people tramping around on its grounds.

- The Abbey, a religious retreat which developed quite a raunchy reputation due to "nuns" sitting outside with their habits hiked up while they smoked in between filming takes. Fifty years later the real nuns are still bitter.

- The famous glass gazebo where Rolf and Liesl danced which had to be padlocked because clumsy tourists kept injuring themselves trying to leap around on the benches.

Yes, Salzburg does not appreciate *The Sound of Music*, but is willing to accept vast quantities of American dollars for it. Mozart alone just isn't a big enough revenue stream.

It was also in Salzburg where we ate in the same restaurant frequented by Emperor Charlemagne 1200 years ago on his tour of world domination in AD 803. He ordered the wienerschnitzel.

And that's the thing about Europe. Everywhere you go you find History, Art, Architecture, Culture and piles of rocks labeled Roman Ruins. We don't have stuff like that in the US of A and if we did we'd have "revitalized" it into a parking lot.

Another thing that's different is that American mountains are composed of stony slopes, scraggly brush, diseased forests and a sprinkling of broken beer bottles whereas in the Swiss Alps mountains are composed of lush, velvet green grass adorned with sprightly non-corn-fed cows capable of standing and even trotting on a hillside without toppling over.

Europe boasts several inventions we found fascinating such as a fantastic train system, amazing architecture, windows that open from the top, bottom and side, square toilets, the bidet and cars small enough to accommodate two people but not with a sack lunch.

However, in spite of all this forward thinking there are still a few concepts that elude them, for example:

- Shower curtains— I can't even begin to imagine why this fairly non-technical but very useful invention hasn't caught on in some places.

- The concept of "normal visiting hours" versus the nearly incomprehensible Italian schedules that are generally not followed anyway.

- Sewage systems that can accommodate among other things – sewage. The 2004 Olympics nearly brought Athens to its knees due to the sewage system's inability to process – toilet paper!

- On the plus side, Greece has mastered the art of cheap wine. Everybody makes their own and stores it in the refrigerator in gallon-size plastic milk jugs. Plus you don't have to put up with sniffy sommeliers because the only choices are red or white and the vintage is by the month.

- Many cities are super "sophisticated" by which I mean there is a total absence of parking.

Food

Foreign countries also contain vast quantities of foreign foods. In America we tend to stick to the basics like fried chicken, chicken fried steak, French fries, fried onion rings, fried pizza, fried Spam curds and batter-fried butter. I'm not making that last one up. It's always a big hit at the State Fair of Texas.

Lately salads are also really popular here in the states. A health conscious American can awaken from a dead sleep at 3:00 am and begin a lengthy and detailed list of salad ingredients to be included or excluded ending with the ever hackneyed "dressing on the side."

Whereas in Europe they just eat the vegetables without all the lettuce which poses a major problem for the non-adventurous

American palate. Chicken or beef are also in short supply in Europe which does have an abundance of lamb and fish.

Italians, French and Greeks always take lunch with a glass of wine whereas your full-bodied American (especially from the southern climes) wants sweet tea with actual ice cubes floating in it.

Europeans can provide hot tea at the drop of a hat, but iced tea throws them into a serious culinary quandary.

Actually wine is so common in Italy it appears in soft drink dispensers – Coke, Pepsi, Lemonade, Wine. You think I'm making that up but I took a picture of such a dispenser in the Florence train station, which is also famous for gypsy pickpockets.

Then there are eggs... A European breakfast consists of a gynormous variety of meats, cheeses, cereal, yogurt, honey, breads, vegetables, tea, and hard boiled eggs. That's it, no scrambled, fried, poached, baked, shirred, or frittata eggs – just boiled – a situation that throws many Americans into major trauma.

I once asked a short order chef in Israel to sauté an egg sunny side up. When I explained what that meant he looked at me like I had two heads and handed the spatula over to me.

However, Asian food makes European dishes look downright home cooked. They routinely eat things with eyeballs or suckers or tentacles or other flagrantly unacceptable organs still attached.

Our first morning on that continent we met our effusively genial host on the street in front of our hotel. He asked what we'd like to eat for breakfast and I naively remarked that eggs and oatmeal sounded good.

The next thing you know we are sitting in a tiny hole in the wall local eatery so small that the cooks stood outside on the sidewalk and reached the stove through a window.

Moments after being seated, a bowl containing two black balls swimming in some chunky off-white substance was plunked down in front of me. Century duck eggs are aged until they turn black. I turned green.

Asian hospitality is boundless so our host kept ordering breakfast tidbits for us including some gelatinous black cubes of what turned out to be a real delicacy – sautéed pig's blood.

By the way, here's the recipe for century eggs. Insert duck, chicken or quail eggs in a mixture of clay, ash, salt, quicklime, and rice hulls for several weeks to several months. Leave there until the yolk becomes a dark green to grey color with an odor of sulphur and ammonia. Scrumptious!

That was when my Beloved and I realized we would be starving to death during this trip.

Over the course of the next month we consumed an amazing assortment of seaweed, dried fish, dried animal innards, dried hairy ear fungus, frogs, snakes (ummmm fresh!) crickets on a stick, chicken feet (America's primary export) and a variety of even more unsavory tidbits that we have no idea what they were.

The culinary high point was a restaurant filled with aquarium tanks where you pointed to the exact specimen you wanted and ten minutes later it appeared cooked at your table. We generously bequeathed the coveted fish eyes to our host.

That was one trip where we didn't gain unwanted pounds.

So I bet pasta every day in Italy is beginning to sound delicious right about now.

And it is. Everything in Italy is delicious, but you have to be willing to try it. Watching Americans struggle with the salad, chicken, iced tea thing in a country known for its exquisite cuisine made us realize that it's hard for some folks to step outside their culinary comfort zone.

Lodging

Most of Europe was built before the Americans with Disabilities Act, thus things like ramps, wheel chairs and elevators are in astonishingly short supply. And THEY DON'T EVEN CARE!

We once stayed in a many starred hotel in Sienna with a bronze plaque proudly boasting that the building was constructed in 1185 and renovated in 1726.

Even when they do have an elevator it is so microscopic in size it can accommodate only one average sized American as long as he sucks in while the door is closing.

Europeans, Asians and many other countries expect you to be able to carry your own bags and walk up stairs. How dare they? Do they think we're hobos?

They also expect you to share a bathroom down the hall with strangers – although to accommodate the ever burgeoning tide of American travelers, family-owned pensiones are industriously turning closets into "luxurious en suite facilities."

Once we stayed in an attic room so small that my 6'2" Beloved could not stand up straight and was barely able to wedge his shoulders into the shower. Photos available upon request...

The Italians in particular create incredibly stylish yet dysfunctional bathrooms. For example:

- Square toilet and matching square bidet. Imagine trying to situate your roundish bottom on a square porcelain object without falling in.

- Showers with no dish, shelf or any other surface upon which to place even one of the numerous body washes, lotions and potions we desperately need to maintain our naturally soft skin and unnaturally shinny hair. This raises the alarming question: do Italians even use soap?

- Beautiful linen "bath towels" the size and texture of a smallish dish rag.

- A sink with no surrounding surface to accommodate so much as a toothbrush.

- Marvelously comfortable bedding with delightful down duvets – in the middle of summer. Ahhhhhh...

Transportation

Before traveling outside the US, my knowledge of transportation was limited to cars, planes and the occasional subway. But there are an enormous variety of other means of transport to get you from point A to point B.

First and foremost there are legs. They are not a new invention to New Yorkers who trudge around on them all over Manhattan. But in more auto-dependent parts of the country, meaning everywhere except NYC, we are horrified if we have to hike all the way into the mall from the fifth row out in the parking lot.

Supermarkets routinely provide motorized shopping carts for their supersized customers. Baby strollers are large enough to accommodate a family of four, complete with cup holders.

But in Europe there isn't enough room for cars because 800 years ago they insisted on building towns with tiny, quaint, cobbled lanes, perfectly suited to twisting your ankle if you're wearing cute shoes like they show in all the travel catalogues.

In Asia they build cities large enough to comfortably accommodate approximately 20,000 people into which they cram two million. The average apartment size for a family of four in Hong Kong is 600 sq feet unless you are lucky enough to get the deluxe model with a spacious 625 sq feet.

So people in other lands devise all sorts of creative transport. Plus they don't have to drive several thousand miles just to get to work because everything is conveniently located next door.

Most popular are bicycles and little motor scooters. We're not talking Harleys here. No, these are little toy sized Vespas like you see in toddler amusement parks.

A slim woman wearing a business suit and spike heels will motor up, park her scooter, remove her helmet unleashing a cascade of gorgeous hair and violá she transforms into a beautiful sexy business woman.

That's right, you can tell an Italian woman from an American woman because the tall slim Italian woman is effortlessly gliding along the cobblestones in stiletto heels looking hot in the sense of sexy, while the short, squat American woman (me) is lumbering along in bulky clogs looking hot in the sense of sweaty.

However, all these attractive young women morph directly into ancient crones draped in all black. There are no middle-aged looking Italian women.

Then there are cars... On the beautiful island of Santorini, poster child of the Greek Isles, we rented a tiny Smart car which contained surprisingly roomy leg space.

Unfortunately we actually stopped at a STOP sign and were promptly rear ended. That's when we learned that in many countries (including New Jersey) traffic rules are optional.

My back-packing-globe-trotting son and I rented a car and drove all over Israel and Turkey together. Road signs in Israel are printed in Hebrew, Arabic and English.

You know how we have deer crossing signs in America? Well in Israel they have camel crossing signs. Plus it's really eerie to see markers saying things like "Nazareth, next left."

Language

We prepared for our first Italian sojourn by taking a course in the language. My Beloved, the engineer, studied intently, completing homework days before class and constructing spreadsheets categorizing all the irregular verbs by their conjugation and tenses. Sadly, he had no ear for pronunciation.

146

I just learned a smattering of practical phrases, like "toilette?" and "vino blanco, per favore" and my favorite "quanto costa?" which means "how much?" But I said it with such flair that shopkeepers called my bluff and answered back in Italian.

When my Beloved tried ordering a meal in Italian, the waiter stopped him mid-sentence asking "Do you speak English?"

However one time he did successfully press his bilingual skills into service. At closing time an Italian guard was busy refusing entrance to an insistent Japanese tourist who spoke no Italian. Narrowly averting an ugly international incident, he negotiated peace between them in English. Fortunately the exchange involved no irregular verbs.

But his language bloopers are legion. In Spain while attempting to order a "curveza" (beer) he accidentally ordered "Cervantes" (an author.)

In Greece one beautiful morning he wished the bus driver a hearty "calamari" instead of "kalimera" (good morning.) The driver paused and asked "did you mean to call me a squid?"

And that's the thing about Europe, Asia and most of England, everyone knows English because it is the language of finance, air travel and the internet.

Nevertheless, people appreciate it when you reach out to their culture, no matter how mangled your effort might be.

You know the phrase "When in Rome, do as the Romans." Well it works everywhere from Poughkeepsie to Palermo. People expect you to respect their rules and customs.

The way to be a really annoying (and probably unhappy) traveler is to ignore the expected behaviors. For example if someone insists you wear a robe and go barefoot in a mosque, then worry about foot disease later. Likewise, if they kindly ask you to step away from the pictures or stop yodeling in the Louvre, please just do it.

Safety

Travel is really safe as long as you take a few simple precautions depending upon your destination. For example, always pack a flashlight, toilet seat covers and hand sanitizer.

If you're going to Europe it's best to wear a money belt to protect your passport, cash, ATM and credit cards. Hint: you should also wear the money belt UNDER your clothes.

European pickpockets just want to pick your pockets whereas Manhattan muggers want to stab you for making eye contact, so don't forget your trusty can of mace when visiting The Big Apple.

In Miami an AK 47 is your best bet. In Texas you should rent a large pickup truck to fend off unlicensed drivers. And in California be sure to pack your LAPD Badge to show you're one of the team.

Returning Home

No matter how wonderful your destination, it's always a joy to return to your very own home sweet home, even if there are a few surprises. After one trip with a teenager caring for our house we discovered the refrigerator had died, the house stunk of spoiled meat, the front door was standing wide open, and billions of fruit flies had reproduced on a discarded apple core. But it's all good.

Travel Experience Assumptions

ASSUMPTION #1: I want to see new places but I want them to be just like home.

Ludicrous as this sounds, if you listen to most professional complainers, the majority of their gripes center on the fact that things are – pay attention here – DIFFERENT from HOME.

Check me if I'm wrong, but isn't the point of travel to see different things? Things you don't experience at home?

Fact: most of the rest of the world is located outside of your place of residence and somehow in spite of that handicap, people have successfully cobbled together lives of abundance.

Relax and go with the flow – or stay home.

ASSUMPTION #2: Travel is not safe.

Travel is quite safe as long, as you don't walk around with the word "SUCKER" or "wealthy dumb American, please help yourself to my many electronic toys and credit cards" stamped all over you.

Things like a large unsecured purse or bulging wallet hanging out of your back pocket just invite people to relieve you of your burdens. We've found all people (except possibly the French) to be remarkably kind and helpful if you are nice in return.

Ask at your hotel about places to avoid or areas of concern. The truth is that other than petty pick pocketing, tourists around the world are considered a "No Touch Zone" by the local authorities because they are such a major source of revenue.

ASSUMPTION #3: Different is stupid.

Wrong. Your culture is one way to live. There are many other equally interesting ways to live.

Travel is not about looking at unique customs and judging them to be wrong by comparing them to what you know. It's about marveling at the diversity of the people and the creativity of their lifestyles and cultures.

St. Augustine said "The world is a book and those who don't travel read only one page."

If nothing else, seeing other people's lives makes you grateful for the comfort and security of your own.

ASSUMPTION #4: Foreign places should have food I like.

Grow up. You're an adult. The days of subsisting on macaroni and cheese are long past.

Sampling the local cuisine is vital to enjoying new experiences. Sure, it may not be something you want to eat for the rest of your life, but it's worth a try.

Plus, if you're really starving there's generally a McDonalds around the corner, although going to a foreign land and eating only familiar American junk food is – in my humble opinion and I'm trying to be gentle here – STUPID!

Seek out eateries frequented by the locals and you'll discover the best cuisine. If the menu is printed in 14 languages you can be sure you're eating at a tourist trap and the food is mediocre.

ASSUMPTION #5: Foreign hotels are not good.

Rick Steves publishes the absolute BEST European guide books. He espouses a style of travel he calls "Europe through the back door" which means trying to live like the locals.

His theory is that the more people you need carrying your luggage and jumping to your every command, the more you insulate yourself from the "real" country you're visiting.

Branch out from American chain hotels. There are many quaint, comfortable, clean and locally owned lodgings. All you have to do is a little internet research. These days nearly every establishment has a web site with pictures and rates.

Again, trust that the universe is friendly and you will be amply rewarded with kind, interesting people and experiences.

ASSUMPTION #6: I'm afraid I can't get around in places where they don't speak English.

These days you have to go to some seriously remote places to find someone who doesn't speak English. People working in the travel industry such as hotels, restaurants, and tourist sites all know enough English to help you. In fact, they probably speak it better than you do.

You'll be just fine anywhere, unless you're suffering from paranoia and automatically assume every time you hear a language you don't understand you think they're making fun of you (which if you're doing some ugly American thing they might be.)

People are people – wherever you go.

I treasure a golden memory of driving around the island of Crete one Sunday in September, the harvest season. Remember in the Old Testament how Boaz let Ruth glean grain in his fields? Well gleaning is still practiced there.

The already harvested fields were dotted with women picking up leftover crops. On a tiny back road we saw an old woman dressed all in black (the sign of a widow) gathering nuts under the spreading limbs of a huge tree.

We stopped. I got out and walked over. Our eyes met.

"What are you gathering?"

A shrug meaning "No the English I not speak."

I smiled my big white American teeth. She smiled her many fewer yellowed teeth.

She cracked open a shell exposing the juicy flesh of a succulent walnut and handed it to me. As I savored it she nodded appreciatively. Then we both broke into peals of laughter at the sheer joy of the earth's abundance and our personal connection!

I believe the universe is friendly and people are good.

Travel Saving Actions

ACTION #1: Study up BEFORE you go.

It amazes me that people go to interesting places with no forethought or preparation. Even if you're going to a resort to just lie in the sun, knowing how to get yourself from the airport to the hotel is a worthwhile investment of your time.

Visiting famous cities in Europe that house vast amounts of western culture requires more prep than say visiting a national park in the states.

Speaking of America, however, Disney World calls for more research than, say a trip around the world. There's a whole science to avoiding long lines at all Disney establishments so that you can HAVE MORE FUN!!!!

I freely confess maybe we go a bit overboard in the preparation department. For example, before we went to Russia I read about 10,000 pages of biographies about Peter and Catherine the Greats, Nicholas and Alexandra and their untimely demise in the 1917 revolution, Tchaikovsky the composer, Pushkin and Tolstoy the authors, plus the famous Russian novels *Crime and Punishment* and *Anna Karenina*. But that's just me. As a result I know a whole lot of arcane trivia, such as:

- Europe is named after the Phoenician princess Europa of Greek mythology who was seduced by Zeus disguised as a bull. I just hate it when that happens.

- One in 10 Europeans is conceived in an IKEA bed.

- Finland hosts a whole bunch of odd competitions, including mobile phone throwing, air guitar contests and wife carrying races.

- Buddha statues in Thailand look a lot like George Foreman on steroids.

- The famous Oracle of Delphi was probably a lady high from sniffing the vapors of ethylene gas.

- On opening day at the famous Roman Colosseum 5,000 animals were killed. During its history over 500,000 people and a million animals died for sport which is almost as many peeps as Arnold "The Terminator" Schwarzenegger wipes out in a typical afternoon.

- In 1628 Swedes constructed and launched the Vasa, a massive warship which sailed a total distance of four football fields before sinking in the Stockholm harbor. Talk about embarrassing…

- It's illegal to die in Westminster Palace – or Disneyland.

Wouldn't you just hate to be marooned on a boat in the middle of the ocean with me? I would too.

ACTION #2: Make reservations.

Back in the olden days, by which I mean before kids, my Beloved and I didn't believe in planning. In fact, one vacation he couldn't decide where to go, so we jumped in the car, got on the interstate and took the first right. We ended up in Arkansas and had a fine time.

Every vacation we'd spend at least one utterly wretched night in horrible accommodations because we hadn't planned ahead. Most notable were:

1. The Green Mountain Motel in Denver CO which boasted a 1950 TV which was old even for the 70's.

2. Sleeping in a Volkswagen outside of Monument Valley in Utah. We awakened from fitful catnaps with red dust stuck to our teeth.

3. Some god forsaken motel in South Dakota with no air conditioning that smelled horribly of well water. As we lay there sweaty and immobile, a leg on the bed suddenly broke. In total silence we continued to lie at a slant until without a word we arose and departed. It was 3:00 am.

Post children, however, everything changed. It's okay to be miserable and stupid in your twenties, but after you've experienced the joy of childbirth and the total lack of cooperation from a bawling infant, you tend to become somewhat panic-stricken about RESERVATIONS!

Now my Beloved would no more set foot outside the house without a complete itinerary carefully bound and color coded than he would consider stabbing himself in the eye with a fork.

I don't recommend planning out every little itty bitty detail because that makes you anal retentive types even more obsessed with being "on schedule." Just make sure you have a decent place to sleep every night.

Now that we're planning trips for family and friends, we recommend the following daily schedule:

- Organize only one group expedition or tour of something big or remarkable each day.

- The rest of the day is free time on your own for peeps to break up and explore or shop or sleep or whatever.

- Dinner together to talk about the day's discoveries and hang out.

It's a system that works well.

ACTION #3: Invest in well-respected tours of major sites.

In famous or historic cities investing in a general tour first will help you get familiar with the landscape. Then you can branch out to see the individual sites that most interest you.

We steer clear of big bus tours and instead seek out smaller, private walking groups led by local guides for several reasons:

- You'll get a better taste of the uniquely special, quaint spots that make the city wonderful. For example, our guide in Salzburg suggested a local monastery beer garden located under ancient spreading chestnut trees and frequented by the locals. Totally hidden from public view and inaccessible to a big bus, it was a spectacular find!

- We highly recommend www.ContextTravel.com for tours of major cities and sites in America and Europe. They're designed for people who want to learn, not shop and are led by doctorate and masters students in a relevant discipline.

- Giant and famous museums have private tours. In Europe local guides will meet you at the door asking if you would like a tour. Trust them. In order to even stand inside the museum they must be licensed. For example in the enormous Prado in Madrid a guide took us to the ten best pieces and within two hours we felt we understood so much more about what makes art great.

- Private guides will take you directly inside, bypassing the huge lines of less-prepared travelers standing outside. Guide books talk of a three hour wait for the Vatican Museum. Once inside you're overwhelmed by the crowds and sheer quantity of things to see. How can you expect to even find the truly great exhibits without help?

- Personally, I want to know what I'm looking at instead of just wandering around thinking "Oh, that's a pretty picture. And there's another pretty picture. And another one…"

- Be sure to stop by the Visitors Center at all national parks to get maps and information.

You've spent a lot of time and money to travel to your destination, it's ridiculous to skimp on finding out about and appreciating the very things you came to see.

ACTION #4: Pack light.

The more stuff you're dragging around, the more your stuff drags YOU down. Don't take all the clothes you own. And leave all the really cute but seriously uncomfortable shoes at home.

The current style of despicably casual fashion works in favor of travelers these days. Unless you're taking high tea with the Queen you really don't need dress up clothes, I don't care what the travel catalogues say. What gets you through the day will get you through dinner as well.

With practice I've learned to travel for over a month carrying only a 21 inch roll-aboard suitcase and a very small backpack. We just do a little laundry every six days or so.

If you think traveling that light is incomprehensible, go to www.RickSteves.com and study his packing tips.

Actually I carry the same size suitcase whether I'm just staying overnight on a business trip or setting off for six weeks on another continent. The only exception is maybe on a cruise because you have to have all those evening outfits with matching shoes and purses and tiaras.

ACTION #5: Go someplace you've never been before.

Travel is the only thing you buy that makes you richer.

It teaches you to be less cowardly, more confident and more willing to risk stepping outside your comfort zone in other areas of your life.

Now that our kids are adults with families of their own, we want to spend time with our grandkids in interesting places but we need their parents with us to do all the hard work of cleaning them up and maintaining their civilized behavior.

The solution is simple. We now engineer family vacations utilizing the time-tested principle that if you, the grandparents, pay for it – they will come.

In summary, we believe travel creates the most vivid memories of your life. It also makes you wiser and braver. So get out there and embrace the rich diversity of our world!

Stop complaining about
the potholes and
celebrate the journey

Wasting Away in Boomerville

"Never take life seriously.
Nobody gets out alive anyway."

Anonymous

News Flash: Baby Boomers are aging.

Baby Boomers were spawned by sex-crazed GI's returning home from World War II. Sometimes referred to as "the pig in the python" because the demographic bulge of their sheer numbers, 76 million to be exact, caused the earth's rotation to shift, and in 1987, they declared themselves "The Official Center of the Universe."

Their parents, known as The Greatest Generation because they stoically survived The Great Depression and The War to End All Wars without complaining, sacrificed everything to create a perfect world for their progeny who in turn became known as Boomers, the most affluent, healthy, well-educated and self-absorbed generation in history.

As they moved through the snake, Boomers invented things like bell bottom pants, disco, SUVs, Farrah Fawcett, hacky sack, entitlement, liposuction, Viagra, and Bagel Bites. In turn, Boomers set off a veritable wellspring of narcissism in the form of Gen Xers, Gen Y, and Generation Text or for short, Millennials.

I am a proud member of the Boomer class of '47.

As a Boomer I spent my entire K-12 educational career outside the main school structure in portable buildings we called The Shacks. Apparently educators in the 50's did not have access to arithmetic whereby they could calculate that if a bazillion kids entered the first grade, then six years later a bazillion kids would enter the junior high. Some of these "temporary buildings" are now designated historical landmarks.

Today Gen X and Y parents are convinced that education delivered in temporary shelters constitutes child abuse and will most certainly wreck their kid's chances of getting into Harvard. These parents have not yet realized that their precocious offspring, despite receiving the most expensive education ever devised by man, will grow up to be claims adjusters.

As teenagers, Boomers dissatisfied with being given every possible advantage, rebelled by becoming Hippies. First, they refused to cut their hair, causing apoplectic dismay for their more conventional parents. They followed that up by roaming the country in VW busses with flowers painted on the side, searching for love, peace and good pot. Time passed.

One day, they got tired of waking up with lice in their hair and decided to become Yuppies.

Young, upwardly-mobile professionals are to materialism what conspicuous is to consumption. After first scorning their parents' Beaver Cleaver existence, they lunged into an über-acquisitive lifestyle, seeking high quality goods just reeking of excellence and exclusivity such as pain-free exfoliants, organic baby wipes, high-fiber yogurt, low-fat cheesecake, breast implants, and imported dental floss.

They birthed and pampered trophy children, scarfed down trillions of Big Macs, fostered a world-wide epidemic of obesity, and divorced each other at an astounding rate. This intense spotlight on self-importance is epitomized by the magazine industry's deterioration from *Time* to *People* to *US* to *Self*.

And now of course *AARP*.

As the pig nears the irritable bowel of the snake, Boomers remain a force of nature: conservative, overweight, and anti-everything.

In typical Boomer fashion, we self-righteously complain about how kids today have no respect for their elders while conveniently forgetting our noble generation gyrated to Elvis, set fire to campus effigies, rolled in the mud at Woodstock and committed unspeakable acts in the back of our parent's Buick.

Boomers are currently retiring at record rates, leaving gaping holes in the workforce that no combination of Gens X, Y, Text, and Millennials (showing up three days a week with six months off to go find themselves) can fill.

And what do Boomers want in elderlyhood? They want to redefine it as "midlife."

For many of them, age 60 is the new 40. Sadly, for the rest, 60 is the new 80 and they're regretting all the beer, pizzas, drugs, and STDs of their youth.

Plus, those stylin' tattoos are beginning to look like so much crumpled newspaper.

Boomers, always an economic stimulus package of seismic proportions, are being serviced by many emerging industries, such as:

- The Life Coaching industry to help them ponder the big "what's next?" question

- The Financial Planning industry to cobble together some kind of retirement nest egg from the $307.21 Boomers managed to save

- The Cancer Scare industry to issue frightening daily reports proving the Big C lurks in everything from sherbet to Sponge Bob Square Pants

- The Grandchildren Rental industry to open all their medications' child-proof caps

- The Harley Davidson Leather Skin and Garments industry to transform innocuous Walter Mitty types into fire-breathing, tattoo-infested, intensely threatening packs of elderly nomads wandering the earth in search of – who knows what

- The Medical Waiting Room Industry where convicted felons are sentenced to hard labor listening to Boomers complain about gum disease, joint pain, bladder malfunction and hemorrhoidal swelling

- The Botox Disfiguration industry to freeze their faces into an inviting and natural looking expression resembling The Joker in *Batman*

- The Erectile Dysfunction industry to help them get it up, and if it lasts more than four hours, get it down again

- The Medicare, Social Security and Obamacare Explanation industry, to clarify any questions that might arise about these government services. This industry is based in India and staffed with helpful individuals named Jennifer, Jason and Abraham Lincoln.

Back in the olden days when people retired they generally had the common decency to go home and die a couple of years later.

But nowadays, Boomers expect to live on – and on – and on. Scientists predict Boomers will live 10 to 15 years longer than their parents. That means the world is stuck with us for 40 more years. In fact, by 2050 there will be more little old ladies over the age of 100 than all other females ages 0 to 5.

And sadly, I'll be one of them.

Women in my family live to 100 with no medical intervention, so I'm staring down the barrel at 115. Have you seen what 100 looks like? It's not pleasant. Like my mother, even when I go to the grocery store I'll be clutching my DNR (Do Not Resuscitate) in my bony, liver-spotted hands.

But unfortunately I won't die of a resuscitation-related condition. No, that would be too kind. I'll just lose my mind, eyesight and bladder control. Depends will become my panties of choice.

A month ago at my last physical, the conversation with my doctor went like this:

Doctor: "Your cholesterol is too high."

Me: "Woo Hoo! At last! A medical condition that might take me out!"

Doctor: "Let's test to see if your arteries are clogged."

Me: "Gosh, I really hope so!"

The Good Doctor hustled me over for an immediate CAT scan to measure the quantity of waxy buildup in the various ventricles of my heart. The resulting score could be from zero (meaning your pipes are squeaky clean) to 1000 which means a heart attack is in progress.

Rats! I scored a zero. There goes my chance for quick death via a good, old fashioned, garden-variety heart attack.

Because we're stuck on this earth for such a long time, my Beloved decided "we" needed to start working out so he (as any respectable engineer would do) began constructing a massive data analysis program to select the perfect gym for us. The spreadsheet calculated many important metrics such as:

- number of machines compared to classes offered

- free towels or bring your own

- Cost per minute of exercise compared to projected pounds lost

With priority list in hand, we began site visits.

First up was Jake's Pump 'n Bump located several suburbs away. As we sat in traffic for 45 minutes trying to reach it we discovered a new critical rule of thumb: the gym must be situated no more than ten minutes from your house. We never made it to Jake's.

Next we visited a nearby Curves facility where my Beloved was refused admittance on the grounds that he wasn't a female. Rule #2: make sure you fall within the gym's target market.

Third up was 24 Hour Fitness where a muscle-bound, steroid-enhanced trainer named Apollo gave us the tour. Every client looked as if they were training for a triathlon. Rule #3: determine whether the gym's clients are your kind of peeps.

Next stop was LA Fitness which claimed a high-machines-to-classes-ratio. The facility was a real meet-and-greet, shop-for-a-date neighborhood place jammed full of slim, happen', spandex-clad twenty-somethings.

I wasn't wild about running into my friends and neighbors at 6:00 AM before all my natural beauty had been glued on for the day.

Finally we arrived at our last choice on the list, the Herman T. Crumpitt Activity and Cardio-Vascular Exercise Center of Mercy Hospital or the HTCACVECMH for short. The facility was jammed with gray-haired athletes on walkers toting their oxygen machines. We felt right at home.

Ultimately the decision came down to whether we wanted to be the oldest, most wrinkled sportspersons among the spandex-intensive crowd at LA Fitness or the youngest, most attractive and healthy participants at the HTCACVECMH. We chose the geezers.

Plus the HTCACVECMH boasted not one – but TWO – emergency crash carts!

Many Boomers think retiring means they can sleep until noon and then play golf for the remaining portion of their natural lives. As actual retired people, they're discovering that this lifestyle is intensely boring.

Hard-charging, over-achieving, Type A personalities quickly tire of so much relaxing and start looking around for something more purposeful.

Of course, the first things males tend to latch on to are the home improvement projects they never had time for before. They go to the giant home center store and return with a manly tool belt roughly the size of Kansas laden with many shiny new devices.

Next they purchase vast quantities of "materials" which they bring home and begin inserting in and around the house. Frequently, however, halfway through a "project" they lose interest and begin another "project," causing visitors to wonder, "Were these home repairs installed by vandals?"

Once all the "materials" are more or less attached, they move on to rearranging their wife's kitchen cabinets, pantry, linen and clothing closets. Along the way they share many helpful but unsolicited tips about how the wife could do the laundry, cleaning, vacuuming, cooking, and shopping more efficiently.

Not surprisingly, many newly retired husbands are found lifeless and cleavered in the head by a spatula.

And what does a female retiree do? Everything she was doing before plus cleaning up the spew effect that follows her retired husband on his many projects.

After several months of living the dream together 24/7, many wives fall down on their knees and beg their retiree to get out of the house. Since he's bored too, he decides to do something to "give back" – give what to whom is unclear, but it preferably involves power tools.

About this time his lovely bride, who is equally bored, decides it is now time to start traveling the world. Together they pour over beautiful travel brochures full of healthy, vibrant, intensely sophisticated people casually sipping champagne (always champagne) overlooking gorgeous and amazing sights. Inspired, they book their dream cruise to Alaska.

For entertainment, the wife spends weeks, even months assembling just the right collection of statement clothing for this exciting vacation, classy garments that will fit in with the beautiful people onboard.

She frets over whether to order the Bon Voyage Champagne Basket or the Nuts 'n Such Snack Pack delivered to their spacious veranda suite.

She carefully selects new luggage, a set of nesting suitcases large enough to comfortably accommodate the lawnmower with room for the edger as well. It is only at the airport check-in counter when they are slapped with $385 in overweight baggage charges that it dawns on her perhaps smaller bags would have been preferable. The shoe suitcase alone weighs 77 pounds.

Undaunted they arrive at the pier, powdered, puffed and resplendent in full cruise attire, but while boarding the ship they are rudely jostled by what appear to be gypsies and hobos. Having seen *The Titanic*, she reasons those folks must be in steerage.

Eagerly our dewy-eyed duo arrives at their "spacious veranda suite" which turns out to be about the size of a large Subaru.

Still nervous about impressing "the beautiful people" our overly-prepared couple climb into full evening attire for the special seating at dinner.

To their horror, the elegantly chandeliered dining room is crammed full of large, loud, tacky tourists hunched over their plates like grizzly bears ripping open a carcass.

Slowly, our precious pair comes to the disappointing realization that there are no beautiful people on this cruise. Their wardrobe declines to the point that they unabashedly roam the ship in their pajamas.

Back home however these minor disappointments fade, much like the pain of childbirth, and are replaced by fond memories of all-you-can-eat buffets, the Grand Chocolate Extravaganza, and gambling the hours away in the smoke-filled casino.

Wearing a souvenir T-shirt that says "Save the Whales – Trade Them for Valuable Coupons," they book their next adventure cruise in the Mediterranean.

Eventually Boomers discover that expensive travel experiences, though enjoyable, only fill about a month a year. What to do with the other eleven?

How about reveling in the role of wise Matriarch and Patriarch of the family, dispensing wisdom and doting on grandchildren? There's just one little problem – finding some acceptable family upon which to dote.

Although Boomers took their parenting responsibilities very seriously, the actual product they produced now falls into one of three categories:

- Offspring that grow up, get married, have children, get divorced and return home dragging behind them a raft of snot-nosed, mal-adjusted difficult people, large, highly emotional, stress-incontinent pets, massive credit card debt, tax encumbrances and no job. Frequently these "children" cannot be sandblasted out of the house for many years.

- "Trophy children" are the well-rounded, expensively educated individuals who leave home in search of lifelong fulfillment and the perfect mate, but since they rarely find mates capable of matching their own personal excellence, instead they specialize in collecting divorces and degrees, while producing no children.

- Occasionally a Boomer gets lucky with a normal, well-adjusted child who grows up, gets married and provides grandchildren, but unfortunately lives in a city that can only be reached via an airplane ticket costing many hundreds of dollars.

My Beloved and I were blessed with two normal daughters and one "trophy child" named Jeff who slowly matured into a highly educated renaissance package of a person and since graduating high school has:

- Obtained bachelors and masters degrees in philosophy.

- Taught elementary school in an outlying NY-based colony named Brooklyn.

- Trekked the 1,000 mile El Camino de Santiago pilgrimage.

- Meditated in a Zen Monastery in Sonoma Valley CA for 2½ years.

- Backpacked alone around the world for a year starting in Kathmandu, Nepal.

- Currently lives and works in Abu Dhabi, UAE, which is located a short hop from his favorite ashram in India.

- Changed his name from Jeff to Mandala which in Sanskrit means "Embrace the Universe." As a result I've changed my name to Momdala which means "prematurely gray and old as the Universe."

Thankfully, our more traditional daughters have married wonderful wage-earning, tax-paying guys who generously stepped to the plate, performed their reproductive duty and co-produced four lovely grandchildren, a girl and boy in each familial unit.

Being a grandparent is fantastic. For starters, the gestation period is a stretch mark and puke-free experience. Instead you simply occupy yourself for nine months selecting your grandparent names.

We are Lolly and Pops.

Lolly and Pops now show up at fairly regular intervals to impart wisdom and rules of appropriate etiquette to these newer family members, many of these rules their stern parents have neglected to cover. Some life lessons include:

- Smack Time - Grandchild jumps across the sofa, lands on Pops who tickles the bejesus out of said child's ribs, who then jumps off, runs screaming through the house, returns to the sofa and repeats the whole process at least ten times

- Monkeys Jumping on the Bed - Jumping on the bed until someone either falls off or sustains a major head injury

- Stinky Feet - Taunting adults with stinky feet remark, requiring the grandparent to commence examining said feet in such a manner that earsplitting screams can be heard in a neighboring county

- Disney Discovery - Endlessly viewing Disney movies about princesses and true love's first kiss to really screw up the child's future adult relationship expectations. And of course, developing an enduring love of, infatuation with, and consumer demand for all things Mickey.

As can be seen from the above list, many behaviors with Pops involve a great deal of personal violence. After several hours of such scrimmaging, Pops hands over the limp, exhausted, sweaty, over-stimulated bodies of these innocent children to their parents who must deal with the meltdown aftermath.

The mothers are not amused.

Yes indeed, grand parenting is great fun.

Aging can actually be a time of renewal and self-discovery. We're super glad we're at this stage in our lives.

Since you'll be wearing Depends anyway, laughing uproariously the pitfalls is the absolute best way to age gracefully.

It sure beats the alternative.

Age Limiting Assumptions

ASSUMPTION #1: Retirement means no more stress, just doing whatever you want whenever you want.

Sounds great, right? Wrong! Many retirees, devoid of outside interests, take a long time and a lot of energy to think of something to do besides sitting around doing nothing.

Actually, if you sit around doing nothing for too long, you'll inadvertently start doing something in the form of developing an exciting career as a full-time patient.

ASSUMPTION #2: I can quit learning now.

Regardless of age or socio-economic persuasion, people who regard learning as work are idiots. Retirement is the perfect time to start filling your mind with all kinds of new, interesting and fascinating factoids with which to amaze your family and friends.

Besides, you'll be able to have more enlightening and humorous conversations with yourself as you begin losing your mind.

ASSUMPTION #3: If I get sick there's always a pill to fix everything.

Yes, pills are good, but health is better. Now is a great time to start taking care of your body.

Since starting an exercise program three years ago, my Beloved and I now enjoy biking together. I use the term "together" loosely because we depart the driveway at the same time and remain within visual contact for the first five miles, but then he speeds up and we re-engage back at the house. Still we share togetherness in the form of shopping for technical garments, cycle-related equipment, and sweat.

We've also taken to eating more fruits, vegetables and fish in smaller portion sizes. We're not fanatical vegans or anything but we're both a lot healthier than we were at 60 – or for that matter at 50 or even 40.

ASSUMPTION #4: My kids will take care of me.

Really? You wish to be subjected to the care of the very people you grounded repeatedly, causing them to miss numerous important events such as sneaking out of windows, smoking, drinking and retching until dawn with their friends?

Or maybe they live in the land of Far Far Away and you think they can care for you by phone. Your kids love you but it's up to you to take care of you.

ASSUMPTION #5: The government will take care of me.

Yeah, let's depend upon an organization so disorganized it has already spent our Social Security savings into the year 3007 leaving the entire system flaccid and empty, like much of Congress. Boomers once believed the government would be there for us, but now we know, that just ain't gonna happen.

ASSUMPTION #6: We'll travel when we retire.

Sure you will as long as the 'ol mainframe is in working order. Sadly, for folks who've loaded on an extra couple of hundred pounds, travel to interesting places isn't going to happen because interesting places are generally not ADA accessible. Europe, for example, believes in stairs – lots of them, miles of them in fact – with no accompanying elevators or wheel chair ramps.

For super-sized Americans who consider getting off the bus to be strenuous exercise, this eliminates such destinations as Europe, Asia, Africa, Australia and much of Manhattan.

ASSUMPTION #7: Death is scary.

Boomers are obsessed with not dying. It doesn't matter how pathetic our existence, as long as we just keep breathing. Considering how persnickety Boomers are, I think slow, tedious, mind-numbing decline from an ever growing heap of bodily malfunction is not all it's cracked up to be.

I'd rather stay fit and healthy as long as possible and then make a quick and timely exit.

ASSUMPTION #8: Will? I don't need no stinkin' will!

Yeah, don't bother to sort out your stuff either. As a final departure gift, leave your affairs in a tangled mess for your heirs, forcing them to remember you fondly as the curmudgeon who saddled them with cleaning out the attic, disposing of treasures at the city dump, arguing over assets, suing each other and just generally wrecking havoc on what remains of family unity. They'll love you for it.

So what's a Boomer to do?

Age Enriching Actions

ACTION #1: Get a life while there's still time.

Most of us Boomers are way too healthy to kick back and give up now.

When I was 63 I questioned whether it was time to retire from speaking and coaching. I mean, who wants to listen to an old person? Could my message still be relevant? More importantly, what should I wear to look contemporary but still age appropriate?

Then God sent me a wake-up call in the form of a very clear message that said, and I quote, "It's taken me 63 damn years to train you because you're so stubborn. Get the heck back in the game!"

Life is full of opportunity. You don't have to save the world; you just need to save yourself by bringing good to the world. Here's how:

- Give kindness. Volunteer. Nothing brings more joy than reaching out to help others. Also, do at least one kind thing for a family member, friend or stranger every day.

- Plunge into a hobby. Keeping your hands occupied and your mind busy fights the aging monster on the front lines.

- Stop complaining. It's true that the words "grumpy" and "old" just go together like "tuna" and "fish." I'm discovering that it takes conscious commitment and determination to control the elderly impulse to rant about all things unacceptable – and there are an ever growing number of them. Sort of like seeing dust molecules in sunlight, aging causes you find an infinite number of displeasing things. Fight the habit of remarking on them.

ACTION #2: Replace complaining with laughter.

- Laugh every day. Looking for the funny in all the minor inconveniences ultimately dispels the displeasure. Laugh about the tough stuff. Laughter is the absolute most effective medicine for your body and soul.

- Say please and thank you more. Making a conscious choice to use these two magic words causes your mind to stay alert to the kindnesses of others. It's a great way to stay connected to the world in a positive way.

- Thank your husband for being "your hero" or tell your wife she's still the one who sets your heart to pumping.

A couple of years ago I made the startling discovery that if I used the word "hero," my Beloved would perk up and sweeten up. Likewise, when he glances at me and spontaneously remarks "you're still the girl I love," it makes me melt.

Sincere acknowledgement and appreciation of your beloved strengthens bonds and makes the heart grow fonder.

Not long ago I mentioned the "hero" tip to a friend. Two weeks later she used it when thanking her husband of 33 years for some deed of service and his chest visibly swelled with pride. Ladies, your man wants to be your knight in shining armor and superhero. Give him that gift.

Men, your woman wants to feel beautiful, appreciated and special. Genuine comments will surprise and delight her. As complex and confusing as women frequently are, deep down they just want to feel valued and loved by you. Give her the gift of adoration.

So there you have it – easy to implement tips to improve your life before you finally relax into The Big Barcalounger in the Sky.

You don't have to waste away in Boomerville or anywhere else in life.

Just choose to thrive!

Laughter makes
life richer